Ontology of Legal Contracts

—

Focus on Finance

William S. Veatch

Website: www.mwnmathwithoutnumbers.com
Amazon author page: www.amazon.com/author/williamveatch

WILLIAM S. VEATCH

Copyright © 2016-2021, by William S. Veatch.
All Rights Reserved. Moral rights asserted.

ISBN: 9798458902205

DEDICATION

This book is dedicated to the memory of my parents, Richard and Lorraine, and my brother David; and to my wife Debbie, and our three children Christina, Will, and Margaret.

CONTENTS

	Preface	i
1.	Introduction to Ontologies	1
	1.1. What is an Ontology?	1
	1.2. Defining an Idea by Its Relationship to Other Ideas	2
	1.3. Requirements for an Ontology of the Law	3
	1.3.1. Firm Foundation in Math and Logic	3
	1.3.2. Joint Venture Between Technology and Law	5
	1.4. Goals and Objectives	6
	1.4.1. Standardization	6
	1.4.2. Collection of Data and Data Analytics	7
	1.4.3. Visualization of Data	7
	1.4.4. Data Has Independent Value; The Value Proposition is Not Just Savings Due to Greater Efficiency	7
	1.5. References, Historical Notes, and Further Reading	8
2.	Contracts Generally	10
	2.1. Sentence Outline Structure Common to All Contracts	11
	2.2. Sentence Topics, Functions, and Short Names	18
	2.3. Classification of Ideas (Other Than Sentences)	21
	2.3.1. Classification of Finance Contract Types	21
	2.3.2. Parties	23
	2.3.3. Timeline	24

	2.4.	Three-Party Relationships: Agency, Guaranties, Indemnities, and Vendor Finance	25
	2.5.	References, Historical Notes, and Further Reading	27
3.	Credit Agreements	28
	3.1.	Sentence Ordering Chain	28
	3.2.	Classification of Ideas (Other Than Sentences)	30
		3.2.1. Classification of Loans	30
		3.2.2. Parties	31
		3.2.3. Timeline	32
	3.3.	Loan Specific Provisions	33
		3.3.1. Topics, Functions, and Short Names	33
		3.3.2. Interest Rate	35
		3.3.3. Optional Prepayments	37
	3.4.	References, Historical Notes, and Further Reading	37
4.	Receivables Purchase Agreements	38
	4.1.	Sentence Ordering Chain	38
	4.2.	Classification of Ideas (Other Than Sentences)	39
		4.2.1. Classification of Receivables Purchase Agreements	39
		4.2.2. Timeline	41
	4.3.	References, Historical Notes, and Further Reading	42
5.	Equipment Finance and Leasing	43
	5.1.	Sentence Ordering Chain	43
	5.2.	Classification of Ideas (Other Than Sentences)	44

	5.2.1.	Classification of Equipment Finance and Lease Agreements	44
	5.2.2.	Timeline	44
	5.2.3.	Events of Default	45
	5.3.	References, Historical Notes, and Further Reading	48
6.	Contract Portfolio Data		49
	6.1.	Negotiations: Correlations Between Contract Terms and Customer Profiles	49
	6.2.	Documentation: Comparison of Competing Contract Forms	49
	6.3.	Monetization: Portfolio Diligence for Mergers & Acquisitions, Loans, or Securitizations	50
	6.4.	Generation of Mass Amendments	50
	6.5.	References, Historical Notes, and Further Reading	50
7.	Conclusion		51
	7.1.	What We Have Learned About Creating an Ontology of Legal Contracts	51
	7.2.	Questions to Ask Your Contract Management Solution Provider	53
	7.3.	Next Steps: Where Do We Go from Here?	55
	Bibliography		57
	Index		68

WILLIAM S. VEATCH

PREFACE

This book is the first in the "Need to Know" series of books about AI and the Law. The three books are:

(i) **Ontology of Legal Contracts**: An ontology of contracts describes and classifies the legal concepts used in contracts, and the relationships among those concepts.

(ii) **The Logic of Legal Agreements – Building a Legal Reasoner**: We are beginning to develop software applications that apply math and logic to mimic the way that lawyers think and reason.

(iii) **The Mathematics of Language**: A new understanding of language in mathematical terms has developed in recent years. Natural language processing soon will be transformed to enable the processing of contracts and statutes as math and logic equations.

This series is designed for inhouse lawyers or business executives who have been charged with the implementation of the Digital Transformation of legal documents, including Contracts and Statutes. These books provide the reader with what you "need to know" to have an informed, high-level conversation with the legal and technical Digital Transformation team.

For this book on creating an Ontology of legal contracts, we begin the process of creating a detailed Ontology of contract terms. For those who want to continue the process of creating an exhaustive Ontology for particular contract forms, there is more information available through the author's website: http://www.mwnmathwithoutnumbers.com/home.html ; or work email: bill.veatch@nortonrosefulbright.com .

For the three specific types of contracts that we review in this book, *i.e.*, credit agreements, receivables purchase agreements, and equipment leases, we examine three key categories of provisions in each type of contract:

- Sentences and their Outline Structure, *i.e.*, their order within the contract
- Defined terms
- Other information both inside and outside the four corners of the contract

WILLIAM S. VEATCH

Most financial institutions consider their forms to be proprietary, so we cannot publish them here. We can, however, use a "Short Name" that represents the essence of the Sentence. Each Short Name, *e.g.*, "Choice of Law," is unique within a particular contract, but each well-drafted contract in a particular category will have a version of that Sentence. For example, each loan agreement will have a "Choice of Law" Sentence. This allows us, among other things, to compare forms from different financial institutions.

In this book we focus on Sentences, but in the next two books in the series, *The Logic of Legal Agreements – Building a Legal Reasoner* and *The Mathematics of Language – English Grammar as a Boolean Algebra*, we break Sentences down into their component parts at the Phrase and Core Idea levels.

Our goal is to promote the following:

- Development of an Ontology of the Law with a firm foundation in mathematics and logic
- Standardization of contract terms
- Development of data analytics and visualization tools for large portfolios of contracts

We also want to illustrate the various forms of data and data structures that are used in Ontologies of the law, including:

- Objects and Attributes
- Partitions
- Chains (Ordering and Classification)
- Ordered Pairs (*e.g.*, Relations)
- Ordered Triples (*e.g.*, three party relationships)

Anyone wishing to contact the author may send a message to MWNmathwithoutnumbers@gmail.com.

Disclaimer: This book does not provide legal advice. For legal advice, you must consult with an attorney licensed to practice in your jurisdiction.

WILLIAM S. VEATCH

1. INTRODUCTION TO ONTOLOGIES

1.1. What is an Ontology?

An "**Ontology**" is defined as a set of "**Ideas**" and categories of ideas in a subject area or domain that shows their properties and the Relations between them. Breaking this down further, we can identify the following elements of an Ontology:

- "**Objects**," which are examples of Ideas (sometimes called "classes"), including:
    - Individual Ideas (sometimes referred to as Atoms or Instances) and
    - Sets of Ideas
- "**Attributes**," which are properties of Ideas (sometimes called "slots" or "roles")
    - A single Attribute like "color" may have a range of "**Values**": *e.g.*, color = [red + orange + yellow + green + blue + indigo + violet]. The number of Values is referred to as the "**Cardinality**" of the Attribute, which in the above example is seven.
- "**Relations**," which describe the relationship between two or more Ideas: xRy = x "is related to" y
    - *E.g.*, x "is a wholly-owned subsidiary of" y
    - *E.g.*, Section 1 "comes before" Section 2

An Ontology provides a classification of Ideas, but it does more than that by also providing detailed information about the Relations between Ideas. The good news in terms of building artificial intelligence ("**AI**") software applications, is that there is a highly developed mathematics of Ideas, involving Objects, Attributes, and Relations that allows us to describe these structures with great precision. As the Ontology grows, eventually we have a **"Knowledge Representation Structure"** or **"Knowledge Base"** that represents our understanding of a particular subject area.

In building our Ontology of Legal Contracts, there are three main areas of focus:

- The Sentences of the contract
- The defined terms of the contract
- All of the other information necessary for a complete understanding of the obligations of the parties under the contract

The first two areas of focus are where we spend most of our time in this book. The third area is challenging, because the interpretation of a typical contract depends upon a lot of information that does not appear within the four corners of the contract, such as the dictionary definitions of terms that are not defined in the contract; or the definitions of terms or other requirements that are contained in statutes and regulations. Still, if we work diligently to build our Ontology and Knowledge Representation Structure incrementally, then eventually we will reach our goal of a complete description of the contract terms in a mathematically precise way.

1.2. Defining an Idea by Its Relationship to Other Ideas

Another way to think of an Ontology is as a way to define an Idea by its relationship to other Ideas. Here are the principal ways to define an Idea, that we will explore in this book:

- List of Attributes, *i.e.*, properties; this is the classic dictionary definition of an Idea, or the list of elements that define a cause of action (using AND logic)
- List of Objects, *i.e.*, examples (using OR logic)
- "Cover *plus* a Difference"; *e.g.*, equipment is a type of goods [cover] that is used in a business [difference]
- Relations, *i.e.*, Ordered Pairs. *E.g.*, xRy = The special purpose vehicle "isASubsidiaryOf" the parent corporation.
- Partitions, *i.e.*, the division of an Idea into its subparts.
- Chains, *i.e.*, ordered Sets of Objects or Attributes that define an Idea.

As a result, once we have classified and sorted the Sentences of a contract, the definition section of a contract or statute is often a good place to start when building an Ontology of the law.

1.3. Requirements for an Ontology of the Law

1.3.1. Firm Foundation in Math and Logic

Since one of our goals is to create a software application that is a "Legal Reasoner," we need a firm foundation for our Ontology in math and logic. The author's books listed at the end of this Chapter, together with the books listed in the Bibliographies of those books, provide such a foundation. **Fig. 1-1** shows the basic Boolean Lattice structure that is the foundation for our mathematics of Ideas.

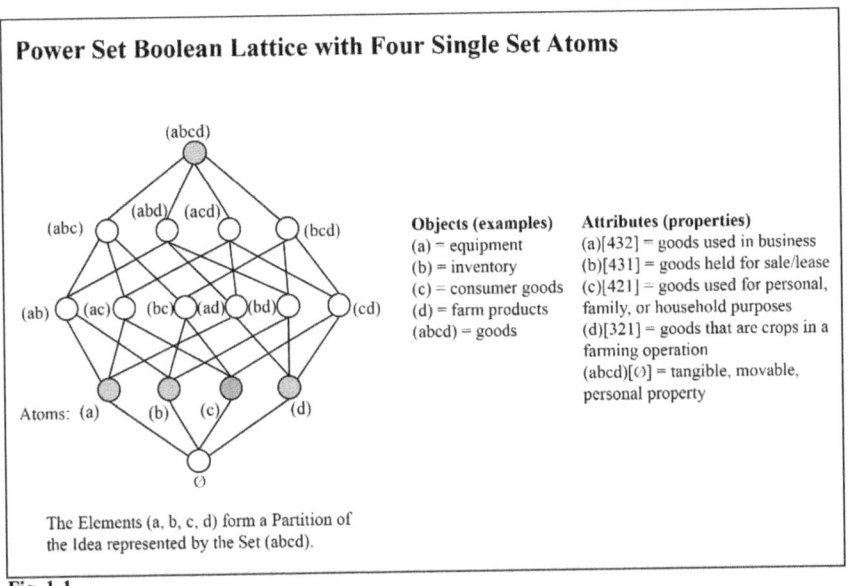

Fig. 1-1

The "Atoms" or fundamental building blocks can be **"Single Sets"** as in **Fig. 1-1** above, represented by (a), (b), (c), and (d); or they can be **"Ordered Pairs"** as in **Fig. 1-2** below as represented by (a,a), (a,b), (a,ab), (b,a), (b,b), (b,ab), (ab,a) (ab,b), and (ab,ab). **"Relations,"** which are represented by Ordered Pairs, are particularly important when creating Ontologies using semantic web technologies like RDF or OWL. The basic structure is xRy, where "R" is a Relation such as the following:

- xRy, where R =
    - "is a Subsidiary Of"
    - "is a Parent Of"
    - "is a Lender to"
    - "is a Borrower from"

(Later, we will see that Relations can be of higher orders as well, such as Ordered Triples.)

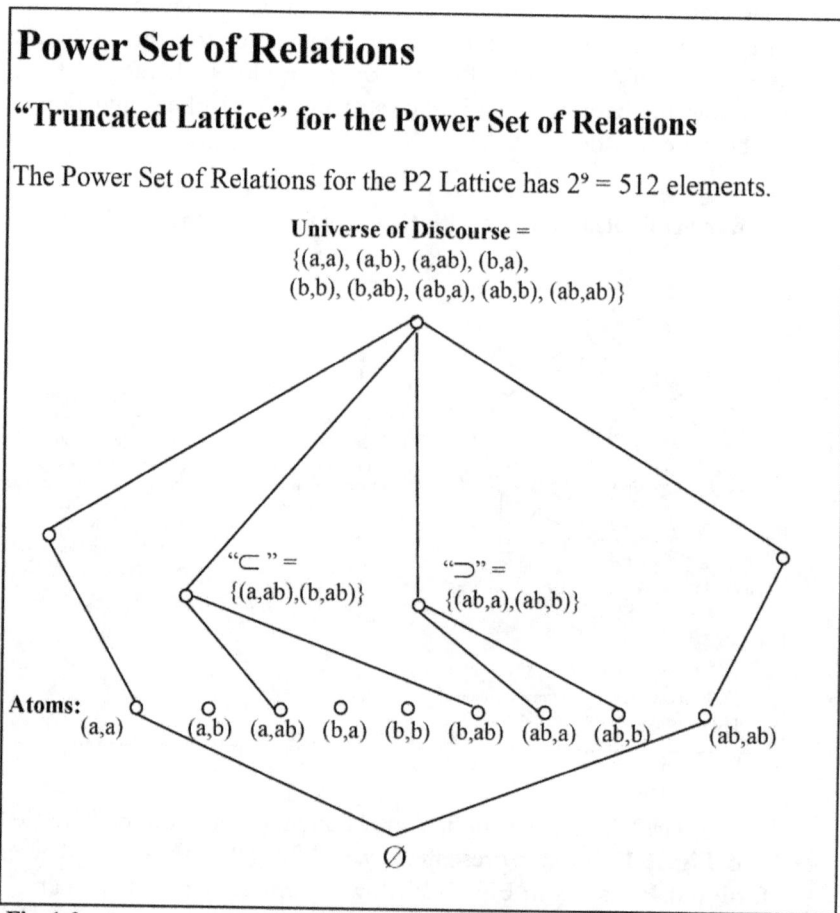

Fig. 1-2

As we build our Ontology, we will rely primarily on the following five math structures:

- **Objects** (examples of an Idea) and **Attributes** (properties of an Idea)
- **Partitions** (also known as Equivalence Relations); *e.g.*, (abc) = (a) + (b) + (c)
- **Chains** (also known as Order Relations); *e.g.*, (a:ab:abc:)
    - **Ordering Chain** (focus is on order, not the "is a" Relation)
    - **Classification Chain** (focus is on the "is a" Relation)
    - **Legal Test Chain** (focus is on the elements of a legal test)
- **Two-Set Relationships** (any two sets are related in one of five ways: Identical, Disjoint, Partially Overlapping, Subset, or Superset)
- **Relations** (Ordered Pairs of Ideas)

There are other mathematical structures besides these five, but these five are more than sufficient to get us started.

It is critically important that we follow the rules of math as we build our Ontology, or we will not be able to take full advantage of our Legal Reasoner, which is the subject of the second book in the "Need to Know" series. By using mathematical structures based on set theory, a computer can process, filter, and sort the data in a variety of ways, including logic equations. *See*, book two in this series: *The Logic of Legal Agreements – Building a Legal Reasoner*.

> *Practical Tip.* Following the rules of math when constructing an Ontology is what enables us to build a Legal Reasoner and other AI software applications.

1.3.2. Joint Venture Between Technology and Law

One of the premises of this book is that the development of LegalTech requires a joint venture between law and technology. A proper Ontology is not just about technology and statistical analysis of contracts and statutes. It is also about the embodiment of quality legal advice in the structured data. A properly constructed Ontology reflects the knowledge and experience of lawyers who have been working with the law for many decades.

Without input from experienced lawyers, there is a danger of a "garbage in, garbage out" phenomenon. In other words, if the legal data is not prepared by experienced attorneys, then the analysis of the data performed by technology, regardless of how sophisticated the technology is, will be flawed. Common problems in sample contract portfolios include the following:

- Grammatical errors
- Flawed logic
- Contract terms that reflect unequal bargaining power of the parties
- Contract terms negotiated by inexperienced attorneys on one or both sides
- Ambiguous terms
- Missing terms

To avoid perpetuating these types of errors in the database of contracts and in the Ontology, it is critically important that experienced attorneys develop the data stored in the Knowledge Representation Structure.

> *Practical Tip:* When creating an Ontology of the law, enlist the help of both technology experts and experienced lawyers.

1.4. Goals and Objectives

1.4.1. Standardization

One of the primary goals of legal technology is standardization. Standardization in turn leads to:

- **Cost efficiency**: Contract review and negotiation takes less time and is therefore less expensive.
- **Improved deal velocity**: Less time is required from the initial presentation of a term sheet to closing and funding.
- **Fewer contract disputes**: If the parties understand what the contract terms mean when entering into the contract, then there will be fewer disputes later.
- **Facilitation of Monetization of Contract portfolios**: Less time is required to review portfolios of contracts that are in a standardized format.
- **Higher Price in a Acquisition**: If an acquirer can determine with certainty that there is limited documentation risk in a portfolio, then the acquirer may be willing to pay a higher price.

1.4.2. Collection of Data and Data Analytics

At present, the most valuable, largely untapped opportunity in contract portfolio management is the collection of Data and Data Analytics. Once we have a standardized classification system for the legal information in contracts, *i.e.*, an Ontology, then we can start collecting and sorting information about contract portfolios in an organized and systematic way.

Without a standardized Ontology, there is no way to compare contracts from different sources and be confident that we are making an "apples-to-apples" comparison. With a standardized Ontology where contracts are classified upon origination, we can compare contracts from different sources in a meaningful way. For this to work, however, we need (i) widespread adoption of a standardized Ontology, at least for particular types of contracts such as Finance Contracts, and (ii) reliable Data input at the time of contract origination. If the contracts are not classified correctly at origination due to human error, the Data will be subject to the "garbage-in, garbage-out" phenomenon.

1.4.3. Visualization of Data

Another benefit to the conversion of contracts and statutes to data is ability to visualize the legal information in new and creative ways. Since the conversion of contracts to structured data is a relatively new field of study, the visualization of contract data consisting of the contract language itself (as opposed to numerical information) is virtually unexplored.

We can visualize relationships among ideas in individual contracts, but the most significant benefit comes from the visualization of data for large portfolios of contracts. We discuss this more in **Chapter 6**.

1.4.4. Data Has Independent Value; The Value Proposition is Not Just Savings Due to Greater Efficiency

Note that some of the reasons for creating an Ontology relate to lower costs of origination or review through greater efficiency, but others are independent sources of value in a transaction. This is especially important to law firms that traditionally bill by the hour. The concern is that: "If the result of implementing technology is the reduction of billable hours, then law firms will lose money." There are several reasons why this line of argument is flawed, including the following:

- **Doing nothing will result in a loss of revenue**: All law firms are implementing technology to one degree or another, so those that fail to implement new technology will lose the business that they have currently.

- **Data is valuable**: The real value of technology and innovation is in Data collection and Data Analytics. This is unrelated to efficiency and is best viewed as an independent source of profit.

  - **Negotiations**: Clients will pay for data that gives them an advantage in negotiations.
  - **Regulatory Compliance**: Clients will pay for information that helps the business stay in compliance with laws in multiple jurisdictions as those laws are constantly changing.
  - **Monetization of Contract Portfolios**: An acquirer or lender will pay more or offer better terms if the risk inherent in the portfolio can be better understood through the availability of Data and Data Analytics regarding what is in the portfolio. If a portfolio owner can demonstrate that the provisions of the contracts are in compliance with all laws, that reduces risk and can result in a better price.

The lesson here is that law firms need to develop alternative billing models that include fees for the licensing of data, not just hourly billing.

1.5. References, Historical Notes, and Further Reading

Tutorials on Building Ontologies

Ontology Development 101: A Guide to Creating Your
First Ontology, Natalya F. Noy and Deborah L. McGuinness
Stanford University, Stanford, CA (1994):
https://protege.stanford.edu/publications/ontology_development/ontology101.pdf

Manchester Family History Advanced OWL Tutorial,
@book{stevens_manchester_2013,
edition = {1.0},
title = {Manchester Family History Advanced {OWL} Tutorial},
url = {http://owl.cs.manchester.ac.uk/tutorials/fhkbtutorial/},
publisher = {University of Manchester},
author = {Stevens, Robert and Stevens, Margaret and Matentzoglu, Nicolas and Jupp, Simon},

year = {2013}
}: http://owl.cs.manchester.ac.uk/publications/talks-and-tutorials/fhkbtutorial/

Foundation in Math and Logic

The foundation in math and logic for this book on Ontologies, is found in the author's previous books listed below and available at https://www.amazon.com/author/williamveatch , and in the books cited in the bibliographies contained in those books:

Math Without Numbers – The Mathematics of Ideas, [Veatch 2016]: This book provides the foundation for a mathematics of ideas based on Set Theory, and in particular the mathematics of Boolean algebras and Boolean lattices.

Propositional Logic as a Boolean Algebra, [Veatch 2017]. In this book, the author develops an interpretation of propositional logic as a Boolean Algebra.

The New Logic of the Law, [Veatch 2018]: In this book, the author develops a new "Logic of Lattices" to apply to the study and practice of law.

Using the Logic of Lattices to Draw Inferences from Structured Data, [Veatch Inferences 2021]: In this book, the author develops a systematic way to draw Inferences from an existing Knowledge Representation Structure.

Demonstration Software Applications

See also, the demonstration software applications at: http://www.mwnmathwithoutnumbers.com/software-applications.html . These are not production quality software applications, but rather are simple applications that demonstrate some of the ideas discussed in the books for educational purposes.

2. CONTRACTS GENERALLY

In this Chapter, we examine the basic outline structure that is common to all contracts. Then, in later chapters we will examine three specific types of contracts: credit agreements, receivables purchase agreements, and equipment leases. To analyze a typical "**Contract**," we start by viewing the Sentences of the Contract as the basic building blocks (or Atoms in math terms) that we need to sort and classify (*i.e.*, with a Partition) and put into a specific order (*i.e.*, with a Chain). We will start with a simple Partition of the Contract into four classes of Sentences:

- Contract: Title: = (Caption + Recitals + Agreement + Signatures)

Every Sentence in the Contract falls into one, and only one, of these four classes. Then, we can create further Partitions of each of the four initial classes.

In terms of the Attributes of Sentences, the most important Attributes in the beginning are the Topic, Function, and Short Name. Every Sentence has a single Topic, Function, and Short Name, so each of Topic, Function and Short Name creates a Partition of the set of all Sentences in the Contract. Many Sentences can have the same Topic or Function, but the Short Name is unique within a single Contract. It is a description of the essence of what that Sentence is about. The Short Name is used as a proxy for the full Sentence in visualization applications; and also to compare Sentences from different Contracts.

2.1. Sentence Outline Structure Common to All Contracts

When we organize Ideas in a mathematically precise way, we use two techniques that are easy to use, but extremely powerful in mathematical terms:

- **Partitions**: A Partition is a division of an idea into subparts. There are two rules that must be followed to create a proper Partition: (i) the division must be exhaustive, and (ii) the elements of the Partition must not overlap, *i.e.*, they must be disjoint. Of special note is the fact that the elements of a Partition are not in any particular order.
- **Chains**: A Chain is a list of ideas in a particular order. In fact, to create a Chain we typically start with a Partition of an idea and then place the elements of the Partition in a specific order.

We will see many examples of Partitions and Chains as we create our Ontology of legal document terms, beginning with the standard outline structure that is common to all contracts.

We start by creating a Partition of the sentences of the contract. *See,* **Table 2-1**.

Table 2-1 – Level One Chain of Contract Provisions

Contract	Level One Division	Comments
Title		*E.g.*, Credit Agreement – Version Number: 1.0. The Title represents the entire contract.
	Caption	The Caption contains the names of the parties to the contract and the effective date of the contract.
	Recitals	The Recitals of Fact section includes background information about the transaction to provide context, and provides a statement of the legal consideration for the contract. The Recitals of Fact, however, do not constitute part of the legal obligations of the parties.
	Agreement	The entire agreement of the parties is contained in this section.
	Signatures	Finally, the parties sign the contract either manually or electronically.

In terms of visualization, our Ontology software application can create a visual representation as set forth in **Fig. 2-1**.

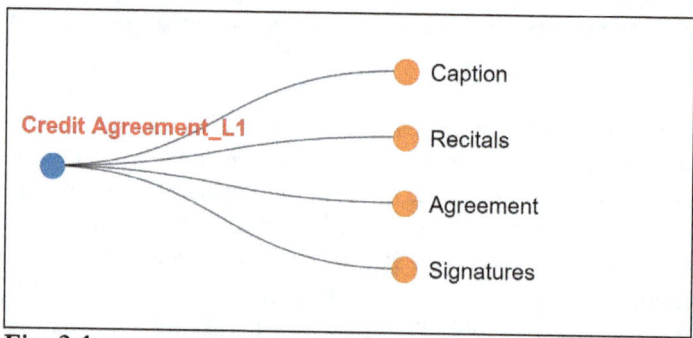

Fig. 2-1

We can write the Partition as an equation as follows:

- *Contract: Title = (Caption + Recitals + Agreement + Signatures)*

This equation constitutes a Partition of the Sentences of the Contract, because every Sentence appears in one of the divisions (*i.e.*, the division into subclasses is exhaustive) and every Sentence appears in only one division (*i.e.*, the subclasses are mutually exclusive or disjoint). Also, if we choose to keep this particular order for the contract provisions, then we also have a Chain. (Note this is an Ordering Chain not a Classification Chain. *See*, [Veatch Inferences 2021] at 106. As a result, we do not apply the "is a" test to elements in the Ordering Chain.) Finally, we also have the beginning of our Ontology of Finance Contracts.

Next, we take one of the four divisions called "Agreements" and break it down further into 12 subparts as set forth in **Table 2-2**. Expressed as an equation, we have the following:

- Agreement $_{\text{Partition}}$ = (Interpretation + [Loan / Lease / RPA Provisions] + Representations + Affirmative Covenants + Negative Covenants + Financial Covenants + Indemnities + Events Of Default + Remedies + Assignment + Definitions + Miscellaneous)

As a technical matter, each division (or Equivalence Class in math terms) begins with the following words: "NOW, THEREFORE, in consideration of the foregoing, the agreements contained herein and other good and valid consideration, the receipt and adequacy of which are hereby expressly acknowledged, the parties hereto agree as follows: ..." To simplify the drafting, however, we typically factor these words out and state them once at the beginning. We will discuss this further in book three in the series: *The Mathematics of Language – English Grammar as a Boolean Algebra.*

Table 2-2 – Level Two Chain of Contract Provisions

	Level 1	Level 2
Title: [Title Value]		
	Caption	
	Recitals	
	Agreement	[NOW, THEREFORE, in consideration of the foregoing, the agreements contained herein and other good and valid consideration, the receipt and adequacy of which are hereby expressly acknowledged, the parties hereto agree as follows:]
		INTERPRETATION
		[LOAN / LEASE / RPA PROVISIONS]
		REPRESENTATIONS
		AFFIRMATIVE COVENANTS
		NEGATIVE COVENANTS
		FINANCIAL COVENANTS
		INDEMNITIES
		EVENTS OF DEFAULT
		REMEDIES
		ASSIGNMENT
		DEFINITIONS
		MISCELLANEOUS
	Signatures	

One thing to note in **Table 2-2** is that the partition of Sentences by Outline Structure does not match up with either Topics of Functions, but rather is a mixture of the two. There is nothing wrong with this as a practical matter. We could organize the Contract Sentences by Topic or Function, but the reality is that with contracts in a data format, we can do this if we want to at any time. That is, one of the reasons for converting contracts to data is that we can reorganize the sentences in the contract any way we want with the press of button.

In **Fig. 2-2**, we have a graph visualization of the nested Partitions, *i.e.*, a Partition of "Agreement" into 12 subdivisions (or Equivalence Classes in math terms), within a Partition of "Credit Agreement" into four subdivisions.

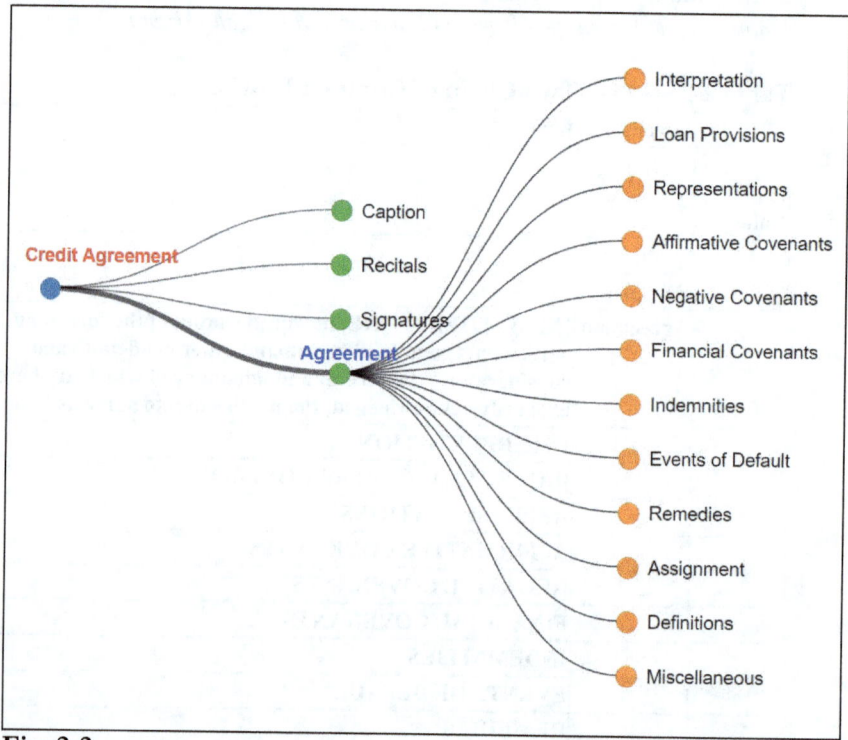

Fig. 2-2

Table 2-3 – Level Three Chain of Contract Provisions

Level 1	Level 2		Level 3
Title: [Title Value]			
	Caption		
	Recitals		
	Agreement	NOW, THEREFORE, in consideration of the foregoing, the agreements contained herein, and other good and valid consideration, the receipt and adequacy of which are hereby expressly acknowledged, the parties hereto agree as follows:	
		INTERPRETATION	
		[LOAN / LEASE / RPA PROVISIONS	
		REPRESENTATIONS	**Borrower makes all of the following representations and warranties as of the Execution Date, the Closing Date, and each Disbursement Date:**
			Existence
			Compliance with Law
			Power
			Authorization
			Enforceability
			No Conflict
		AFFIRMATIVE COVENANTS	
		NEGATIVE COVENANTS	
		FINANCIAL COVENANTS	
		INDEMNITIES	
		EVENTS OF DEFAULT	
		REMEDIES	
		ASSIGNMENT	
		DEFINITIONS	
		MISCELLANEOUS	
	Signatures		

As we continue to break down headings into smaller and smaller subdivisions, you can start to see the pattern. First, we select a heading (or Equivalence Class in math terms) that we want to subdivide (*e.g.*, Agreement of the Parties; or Representations). Next, we create a Sentence to introduce the new subdivision (an "**Introductory Clause**"):

- Agreement of the Parties:
    - "NOW, THEREFORE, in consideration of the foregoing, the agreements contained herein and other good and valid consideration, the receipt and adequacy of which are hereby expressly acknowledged, the parties hereto agree as follows:"
- Representations:
    - "Borrower makes all of the following representations and warranties as of the Execution Date, the Closing Date and each Disbursement Date:"

(As noted earlier, technically, the Introductory Clause is part of each Sentence that follows in the Partition, but, traditionally, we factor it out and state it once at the beginning of the Partition.)

Then, we add the new list of subdivisions. This is the approach that we usually follow when drafting complex contracts. Even simple contracts, however, can (and arguably should) follow this same structure as a "best practice." In this way, we can create a standardized process for drafting contracts that (i) follows best practices in the legal profession, and (ii) follows the rules of mathematics for Boolean Algebras/Lattices, which will allow us to create AI software applications to process the contract information.

If we write the Partition as an equation, we get the following:

- Representations $_{Partition}$ = $(R_1 + R_2 + R_3 + R_4 + R_5 + R_6)$ = (Existence + Compliance with Law + Power + Authorization + Enforceability + No Conflict)

In this way, we can create finer and finer subdivisions until we have classified all of the Sentences in the Contract in a meaningful way. Usually, we like to have fewer than 12 subdivisions in any particular Partition, so a long, complex contract will have a more elaborate classification scheme, with many sub- and sub-subdivisions, whereas a simple Contract with a small number of Sentences will have a less complex classification scheme.

In addition to the "Outline Structure" Attribute, there are many other Attributes of Contracts that we track in terms of Data, including the following:

WILLIAM S. VEATCH

Contract $_{PE}$ =

> **Title/Name:** (Mutual Nondisclosure Agreement + Master Lease Agreement + Credit Agreement + Receivables Purchase Agreement + Other $_{RE}$) x
>
> **Subject Matter:** (Confidential Information + Loan of Money + Lease of Equipment + Other $_{RE}$) x
>
> **Contract Type:** (NDA + Lease: (True Lease + Lease that Creates a Security Interest) + Loan: (Credit Agreement + Promissory Note + Installment Payment Agreement) + License + Receivables Purchase + Other $_{RE}$) x
>
> **Number of Parties:** (1 + 2 + ... Other $_{RE}$) x
>
> **First Party Type:** (Receiving Party + Disclosing Party + Lender + Borrower + Lessor + Lessee + + Other $_{RE}$) x
>
> **Second Party Type:** (Receiving Party + Disclosing Party + Lender + Borrower + Lessor + Lessee + Other $_{RE}$) x
>
> **Drafter of the Contract:** (Receiving Party + Disclosing Party + Lender + Borrower + Lessor + Lessee + Other $_{RE}$) x
>
> **Favored Party:** (Receiving Party + Disclosing Party + Lender + Borrower + Lessor + Lessee + Other $_{RE}$) x
>
> **Stage:** (Form + Bespoke Draft + Instance)

We can define any particular "Contract" by selecting one (and only one) Attribute Value from each Partition in the Partition Equation. For example:

- Contract No. 1 = (Credit Agreement + Loan of Money + Loan + 2 + Lender + Borrower + Lender + Lender +Form)
- Contract No. 2 = (Master Lease Agreement + Lease of Equipment + True Lease + 2 + Lessor + Lessee + Lessor + Lessor +Form)

2.2. Sentence Topics, Functions, and Short Names

In this Section, we examine three of the most common Partitions of Sentences in a contract (in addition to the Outline Structure Partition and other Attributes that we looked at previously):

- **Topic**: This is perhaps the most important part of the Ontology, because this is the information that we return to most often to locate a particular Sentence. Topics include things like interest rate, choice of law, assignments, *etc.*
- **Function**: The "Function" is the role that the Sentence plays in the Contract as a representation, covenant, event of default, *etc.*
- **Short Name**: The "Short Name" is a unique name for a Sentence within a Contract. The value to having a Short Name is in the fact that we can compare two or more Sentences from different contracts that have the same Short Name. The Short Name also serves as a proxy for the full Sentence in Visualization applications.

In this Section, we provide a high-level breakdown of Topics and Functions, but each type of Finance Contract has its own more detailed Ontology. As a result, we provide some examples of a more detailed Ontology in later chapters. (There is a "Short Name" for every Sentence in a Contract, so we do not list them all here. In the companion software demonstration programs, however, we include the Short Names.)

Sentences $_{PE}$ = (Outline Structure) x (Topic) x (Function) x (Short Name)

Topic $_{PE}$ = (Formation + Operations + Termination)

> **Formation** $_{PE}$ = (Formalities + Interpretation + Original Parties + Effective Date)
>
>> **Formalities** = (Authorization + Execution + Delivery)
>>
>> **Interpretation** = (Accounting Terms + Definitions)
>>
>> **Original Parties** = (Lender + Borrower + Lessor + Lessee + Licensor + Licensee + Buyer + Seller)

Operations $_{PE}$ = ([Loan/Lease/RPA] + Amendments + Transfers + Enforcement + Miscellaneous)

    Amendments = (Amendments in Writing + Required Consents)

    Enforcement = (Bankruptcy + Default)

        Bankruptcy = (Involuntary Insolvency Proceeding + Voluntary Insolvency Proceeding)

        Default = (Change of Control + Cross-Default + ERISA Event + Failure to Pay Debts + Failure to Pay Interest + Failure to Pay Principal + False Representation + Immediate Defaults + Judgment + Other Covenant)

    Miscellaneous = (Agency + Communications + Confidentiality + Expenses + Fees + Financial Performance + Investments + Laws + Other Laws + Tax)

    Transfers = (Assignment + Participation)

Termination $_{PE}$ = (Effect of Termination + Term)

Function $_{PE}$ = (Primary + Secondary)

    Primary $_{PE}$ = (Representation + Covenant + Condition + Event of Default + Warranty)

    Secondary $_{PE}$ = (Statement of Consideration + Disclaimer + Definition + Grant of Rights + Waiver + Rule of Interpretation + Mutual Agreement + Direction/Order + Assignment: (Sale + Participation) + Assumption of Risk)

In **Fig. 2-3** and **2-4**, respectively, we have a visualization of the Ontology of Topics and Functions.

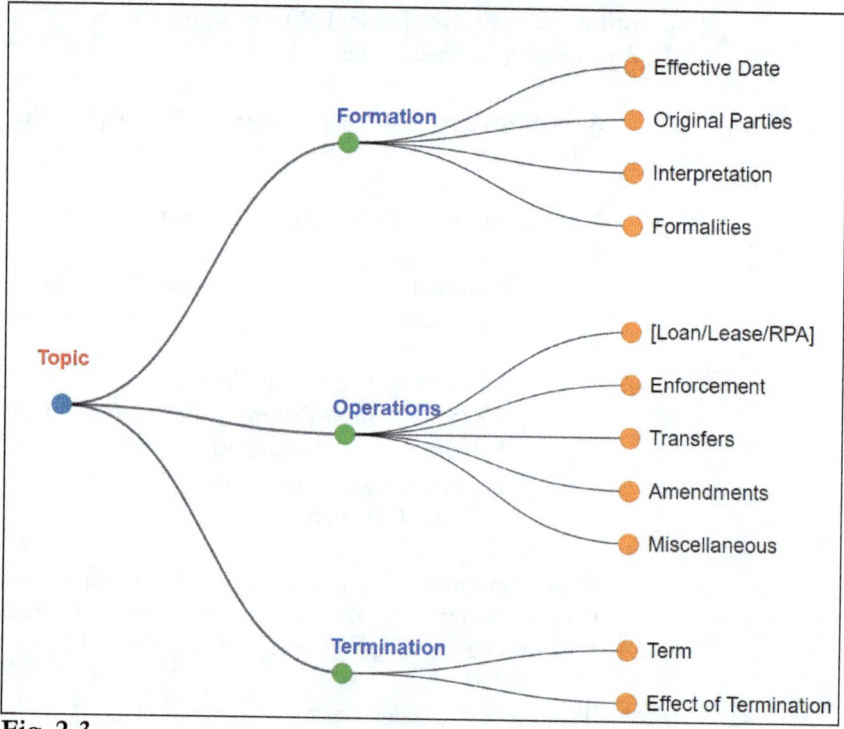

Fig. 2-3

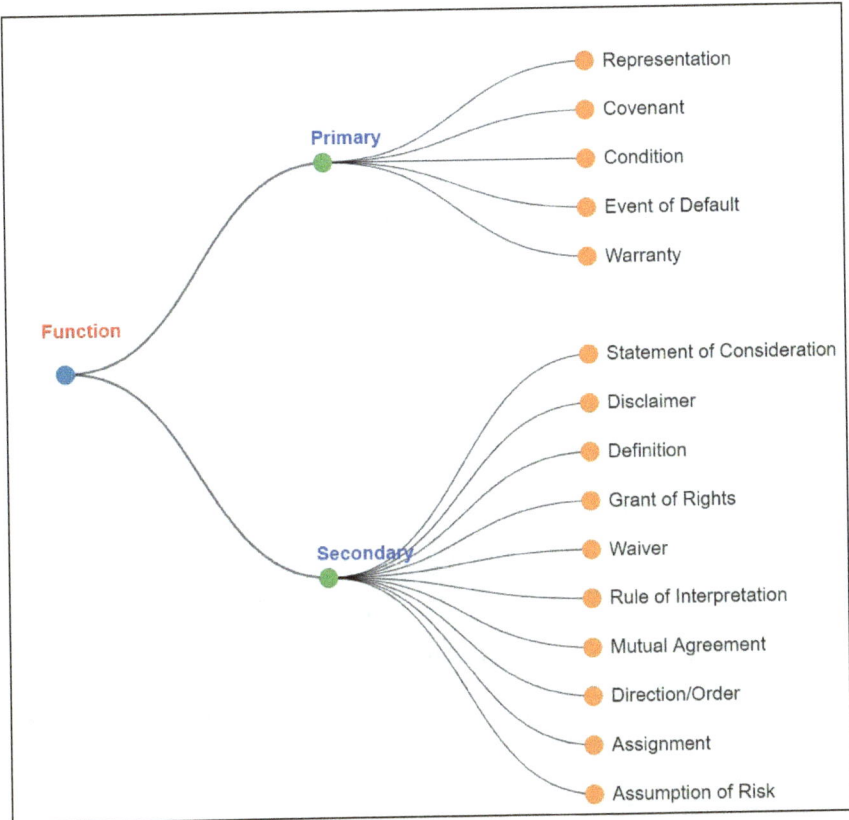

Fig. 2-4

2.3. Classification of Ideas (Other Than Sentences)

In this Section, we begin to look at Atoms that are Ideas in the Contract other than Sentences. Up to this point, we have focused primarily on building blocks or Atoms that are Sentences in the Contract, but other types of Data are equally important, including the Core Ideas that form the Subject and Predicate of a Sentence, the classification of Persons that make up the parties to a Contract, and the Timeline over which a Contract operates.

2.3.1. Classification of Finance Contract Types

In this Section, we look at the classification of finance Contract types as a means of creating an Ontology of abstract Ideas, as opposed to an Ontology of Sentences in the contract. In other words, the building blocks (or "Atoms" in math terms) are Ideas rather than Sentences.

- **Contract** PE =

  Type: (Contract for Goods, Software, and/or Services + Finance Contract)

  o **Contract for Goods, Software, and/or Services** PE =

  Type: (Sale: (Cash Upfront + Installment Sale) + True Lease + License + Service Agreement)

  o **Finance Contract** PE =

  Type: (Loan + Lease that Creates a Security Interest + True Sale of Receivables)

  - **Loan** PE =

    Type: (Credit Agreement + Installment Payment Agreement (IPA) + Promissory Note + Factoring)

In **Fig. 2-5**, we have a visualization of the classification of Finance Contracts.

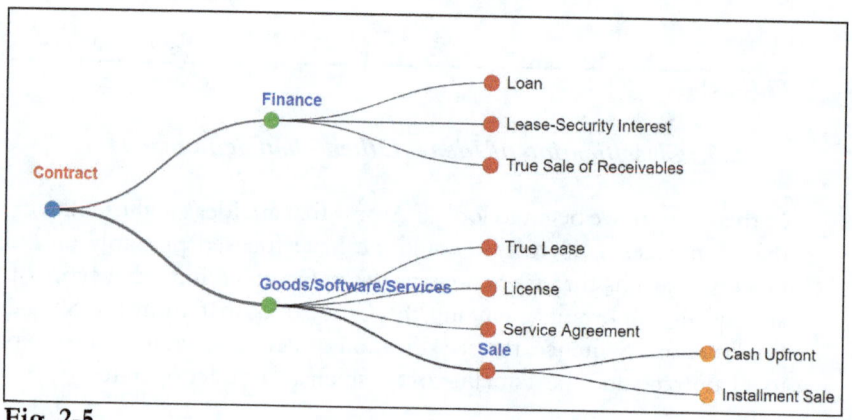

Fig. 2-5

With the Ontology of Contract types, we have a "Subset-Superset" relationship among classes of Objects, where the "is a" relationship applies. For example, the following statements are True:

- A Credit Agreement "is a" loan.
- A loan "is a" finance contract.

- A finance contract "is a" contract.

The distinctions between the various types of Contracts are extremely important as a practical matter, because in some jurisdictions certain contracts, such as a Contract for the sale of goods with installment payments, may not require a lender license or be subject to usury interest rate limitations, whereas a "loan" may require a lender license and be subject to rate limitations.

2.3.2. Parties

We can create a Partition Equation to define a "Party" to a Contract, by listing the Attributes that we use to define a Party, together with a list of the Values that each Attribute may hold.

- **Party** $_{PE}$ =

    Type of Person: (Individual + Entity) x

    Type of Contract: (Loan + Lease + RPA) x

    Role in the Contract: (Lender + Borrower + Lessor + Lessee + Buyer + Seller)

- **Entity** $_{PE}$ =

    Type: (Partnership + Limited Liability Company + Corporation) x

    Governmental: (Government + ¬ Government) x

In **Fig. 2-6**, we have a visualization of the classes of Person that are normally including in a definition of Person in a Finance Contract.

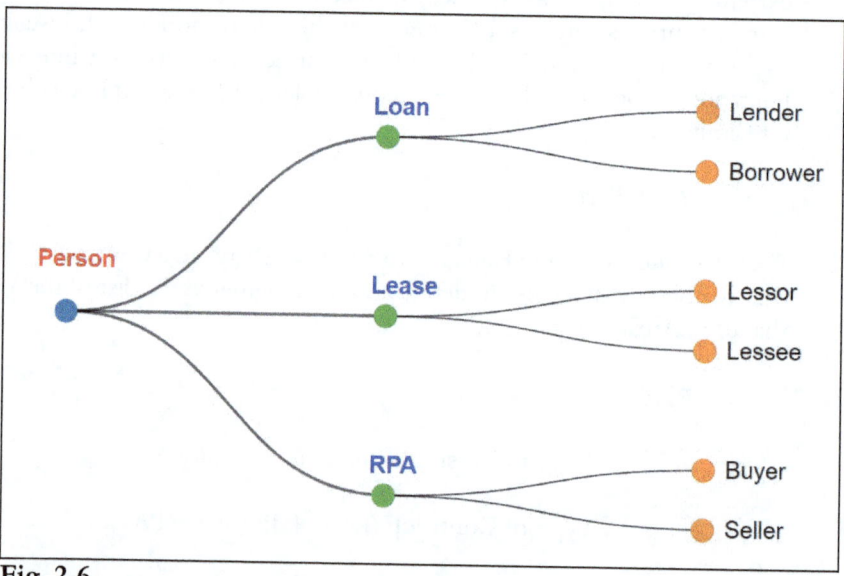

Fig. 2-6

2.3.3. Timeline

The Timeline is critical in any Contract, but especially in a Finance Contract where typically there are numerous payment and reporting deadlines.

- **Timeline Events** $_{PE}$ =

    Type: (Payment + Reporting + Term)

    Payment:

    Type: (Interest + Principal + Fees + Expenses) x

    Frequency: (One Time + Monthly + Quarterly + On Demand)

Reporting:

> **Type**: (Financial + Sales + Customer Data) x
>
> **Frequency**: (Monthly + Quarterly + On Demand)
>
> **Term**: (Start Date + End Date + Extended End Date)

2.4. Three-Party Relationships: Agency, Guaranties, Indemnities, and Vendor Finance

In this Section we look at legal relationships among three parties. Up to this point, we have focused on relationships among Sentences in a Contract or abstract Ideas relating to Contracts, but here we look at relationships among the parties to a Contract and in particular Contracts with three Parties. It turns out that the mathematics of Ordered Triples works well to represent three-party relationships in a mathematically precise way. *See*, **Fig. 2-7**.

Three-Party Relationships - Ordered Triples: Guaranty

A three-party relationship is best represented using an Ordered Triple. The elements of the Ordered Triple are the three Two-Party relationships:

(Borrower-Lender, Beneficiary-Guarantor, Obligor-Guarantor)

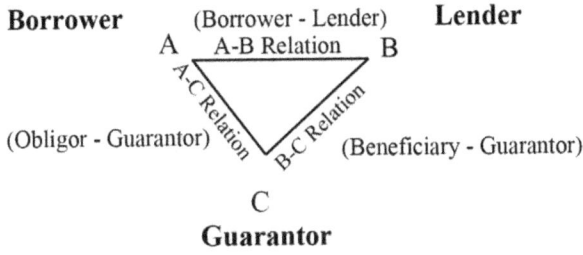

Fig. 2-7

In a bilateral or two-party Contract, we have the following:

- xRy, where R = "is a lender to":
  - Bank "is a lender to" Borrower.

We also have the Inverse Relation:

- yRx, where R = "is a Borrower from":
  - Borrower "is a borrower from" Bank.

Now, we add the party "z" who is a Parent of Borrower and Guarantor of Borrower's obligations to Bank:

- zRx, where R = "is a guarantor of":
  - Parent "is a guarantor of" Borrower.

When we explore Legal Reasoning in the second book in this Series, we will see that it is helpful to express the three-party relationship as an Ordered Triple of Relationships:

- (A-B Relationship, B-C Relationship, A-C Relationship) = (Borrower-Lender, Beneficiary-Guarantor, Obligor-Guarantor)

Along with the names of the Parties, we can store information in our Ontology about both Bilateral Relationships and Three-Party Relationships.

Other common three-party relationships that we find in Finance Contracts include the following:

- Borrower – Lender – Agent
- Vendor – Customer – Lender
- Indemnitor – Indemnitee – Third-Party

See, Using the Logic of Lattices to Draw Inferences from Structured Data, [Veatch Inferences 2021], for more information about Relations from a mathematical perspective.

2.5. References, Historical Notes, and Further Reading

Division/Classification and Order as Studied in Philosophy and Classical Logic

Kreeft, *Socratic Logic*.

Introduction to Mathematical Logic

[Rodgers 2000]

Mathematics of Ideas; Legal Logic

Math Without Numbers, [Veatch 2016]

The New Logic of the Law, [Veatch 2018]

Using the Logic of Lattices to Draw Inferences from Structured Data, [Veatch Inferences 2021],

Relations

[Toth 2020]

[Schmidt 2011]

3. CREDIT AGREEMENTS

In this Chapter, we begin to create an Ontology that is specific to credit agreements. As noted earlier, the easiest way to get started is with a classification of the Sentences in agreement, typically by Outline Structure, Topic, and Function, and then expand to the defined terms in the contract. Ultimately, we will also need to add information from sources outside of the contract to the Knowledge Representation Structure to fully understand the rights and obligations of the parties.

3.1. Sentence Ordering Chain

In this section, we begin by expanding our Outline Structure for the Contract to include loan-specific terms under the "Agreement" subdivision of the Contract. All of the Sentences in the Contract that relate to the specific subject matter of "loans" will be organized and classified in this section. *See,* **Table 3-1.**

Table 3-1 – Level Three and Four Chain of Contract Provisions

	Level 1	Level 2	Level 3	Level 4
Title: Credit Agreement		...		
	Agreement			
		INTERPRETATION		
		LOAN PROVISIONS		
			Commitments	
				Initial Commitments
				Increase in Commitments
				Termination of Commitments
				Sharing of Payments
			Loans	
			Borrowing Procedure	
				Borrowing Request
				Funding
			Interest	
			Prepayments	
			Fees	
			Rates	
				Compensation for Losses
				Increased Costs
				Taxes
				Inability to Determine Rates
				Illegality
				Mitigation Obligations; Replacement of Lenders
				Benchmark Replacement Setting
		...		
		Signatures		

3.2. Classification of Ideas (Other Than Sentences)

In addition to loan-specific Sentences that we classify using the "Outline Structure" Partition and Chain, there are loan-specific Ideas that we can also sort and classify.

3.2.1. Classification of Loans

As is usually the case when creating an Ontology of legal information, we start with a Partition Equation. We ask: (i) what are the Attributes (also known as properties or slots) that we use to classify Loan Agreements; and (ii) what is the range of possible Values for each of those Attributes?

Loan $_{PE}$ =

> **Loan Type**: (Revolving + Term + Swingline) x
>
> **Rate**: (Prime + LIBOR + ABR + SOFR + Other $_{RE}$) x
>
> **Dollar Size**: (Small + Medium + Large)

Borrower $_{PE}$ =

> **Person Type**: (Individual + Sole Proprietorship + Partnership + LLC + Corporation + Non-Profit) x
>
> **Profile**: (Privately Funded + Venture Backed: Early Stage + Venture Backed: Late Stage + Public + Investment Grade + Multinational)

Commitment $_{PE}$ =

> **Type**: (Initial Commitments + Incremental Commitment) x
>
> **Character**: (Term Loan Commitment + Revolving Commitment + Swingline Commitment)

Again, the creation of a particular Ontology is a creative process with many possible outcomes, as long as we follow the rules for creating a valid Partition (*i.e.*, Exhaustive and Mutually Exclusive divisions). There is no mathematical requirement that we all use the same Ontology, but there are practical advantages to doing so, such as the ability to compare documents or simplify diligence in an acquisition, which could result in a higher purchase price. For most businesses, it will likely be most advantageous to use the standardized Ontology, but then also create specific Ontologies that relate to the specific nuances of the particular business. Again, as long as we follow the rules of mathematics for creating valid Partitions and Chains, then we can have multiple Ontologies for the same underlying data; there is no need (from a mathematical perspective) to choose one or the other.

3.2.2. Parties

It is important to track data regarding the identity of the parties, authorized signatories, permitted assignees, *etc.* Tracking Party information is particularly important when it comes time to generate amendments for a particular contract, or mass amendments for a large portfolio of contracts.

Person $_{PE}$ = (Natural Person + Partnership + Trust + Association + Limited Liability Company + Corporation + Bank + Governmental Authority + Other $_{RE}$)

Contract Party $_{PE}$ = (Borrower + Lender)

Borrower $_{PE}$ =

>**Name**: ([list of borrowers in portfolio]) x

>**Type of Person**: (Natural Person + Partnership + Trust + Association + Limited Liability Company + Corporation + Bank + Governmental Authority + Other $_{RE}$) x

>**Stage of Company**: (Private + Venture Backed: Early Stage + Venture Backed: Late Stage + Public + Investment Grade + Multinational) x

>**Jurisdiction of Organization**: (Delaware + California + New York + Other $_{RE}$)

Lender $_{PE}$ =

>**Type**: (Bank + FinTech + Debt Fund)

For any specific borrower, we select one Value from each Partition in the Partition Equation for the Set of all Portfolio Borrowers. For example:

- **Specific Borrower** ~PE~ =

    Name: (ABC Corporation, Inc.) x

    Type of Person: (Corporation) x

    Stage of Company: (Public) x

    Jurisdiction of Organization: (Delaware) x

3.2.3. *Timeline*

Once we know the type of loan and the parties, one of the most important topics to flush out is the Timeline, *i.e.*, What is the closing date? When are payments due? What is the term of loan? For an existing loan agreement, we can read through the agreement and highlight all of the "events" that are contemplated by the loan terms. Some events relate to covenants, such as Payment Dates, whereas other events may or may not ever happen, such as a bankruptcy of the borrower. The Timeline for past events is frozen based upon what actually happened, but the Timeline for future events is undetermined and could take one of many different paths. Therefore, we need to contemplate many different future scenarios. *See*, **Fig. 3-1**.

- **Timeline: Relevant Dates** ~PE~ = (Contract Execution + Payment Dates + Reporting Dates + Early Termination + Termination Date + Extended Termination Date)

The book *Using the Logic of Lattices to Draw Inferences from Structured Data*, [Veatch Inferences 2021] discusses Timelines in detail, including how we can draw Inferences about time from the Data in our Knowledge Representation Structure.

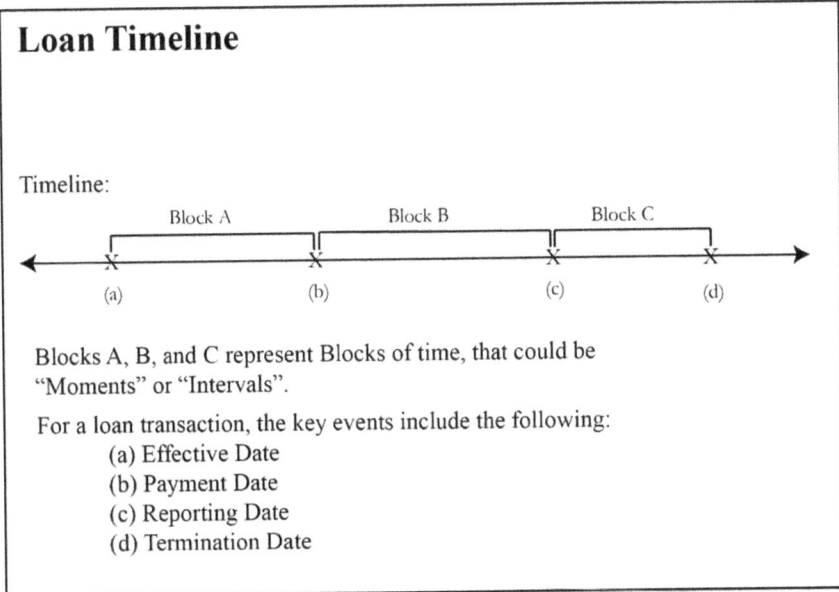

Fig. 3-1

3.3. Loan Specific Provisions

In this section, we examine some of the loan-specific provisions that we include in an Ontology of Credit Agreements.

3.3.1. Topics, Functions, and Short Names

Here, we start with our generic Topic and Function Ontologies, and then expand them to cover selected Topics and Functions that are specific to loans.

Topics $_{PE}$ =

Type: (Formation + Operations + Termination)

Formation = (Effective Date + Original Parties + Interpretation + Formalities)

Operations = (Loans + Enforcement + Transfers + Miscellaneous)

Termination = (Term + Effect of Termination)

Loans PE =

> **Type:** (Collateral + Commitments + Credit Extensions + Defaulting Lender + Funding + Increased Costs + Interest + Letters of Credit + Loan Type + Payments + Revolving Loan + Swaps + Swingline Loan + Term Loan) x

See, **Fig. 3-1**, for a visualization of the Operations: Loans Ontology.

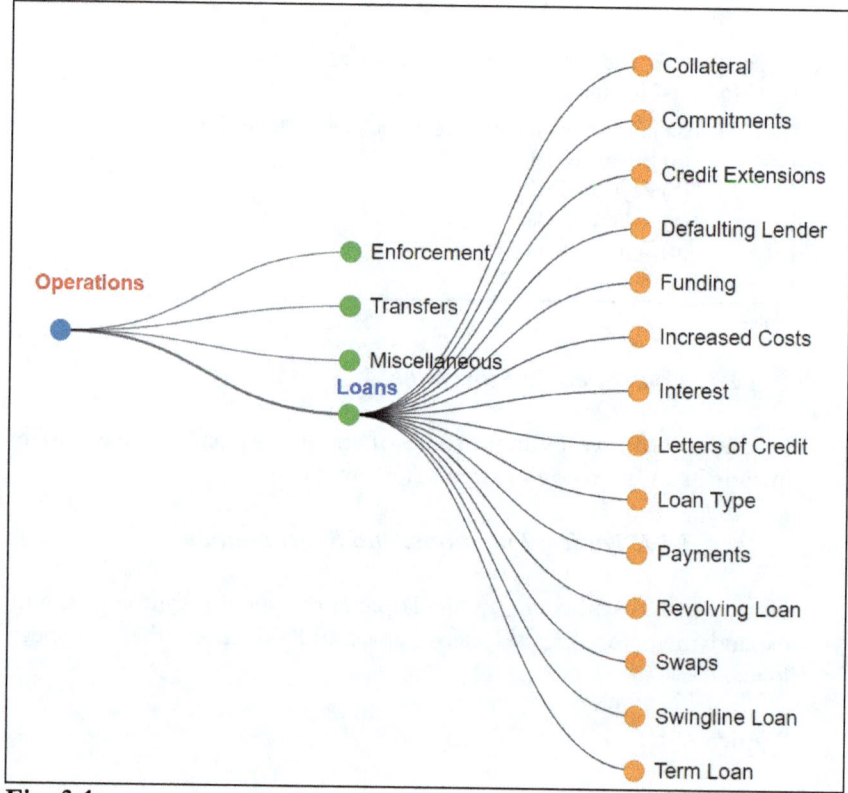

Fig. 3-1

Function PE = (Primary + Secondary)

> **Primary** PE = (Representation + Covenant + Indemnity + Condition + Event of Default + Warranty)

> **Secondary** PE = (Statement of Consideration + Disclaimer + Definition + Grant of Rights + Waiver + Rule of Interpretation +

Mutual Agreement + Direction/Order + Assignment: (Participation + Sale) + Assumption of Risk)

Representation PE = Type: (Existence + Qualification + Power + Authorization + No Contravention + Governmental Authorization + No Material Adverse Effect + Litigation + Other RE) x

Covenant PE =

    Type: (Affirmative + Negative + Financial)

Affirmative Covenants PE =

    Name/Label: (Disclosure + Inspection + Insurance + Use of Proceeds + Further Assurances + Other RE)

Negative Covenants PE =

    Name/Label: (Indebtedness + Liens + Fundamental Changes + Dispositions + Restricted Payments + Transactions with Affiliates + Other RE)

Financial Covenants PE =

    Name/Label: (Net Worth + Interest Coverage + Fixed Charges Coverage + Capital Expenditures + Other RE)

Note that we are not restricted to any one classification system. So long as we follow the rules for creating a valid Partition (Exhaustive and Mutually Exclusive), many Partitions are possible.

3.3.2. Interest Rate

At the time of writing this book, we are experiencing the "LIBOR Transition" where Lenders need to stop using LIBOR as an interest rate in loan agreements, because the LIBOR rate is expected to be unavailable by the middle of 2023. This raises a number of issues for our Ontology of loan agreement terms, but it also provides us with an opportunity to ramp up the development and implementation of a detailed Ontology as a tool to facilitate the LIBOR Transition, and in particular mass amendments that will be required until LIBOR has been phased out completely as an interest rate.

In terms of classification of interest rate provisions, it would be helpful to track all of the following Attributes, together with the Range of Values that each Attribute may have:

- **LIBOR Provisions**: Existing LIBOR provisions and variations
  - Variations of the LIBOR fallback provisions
- **Replacement Rate Provisions**: Proposed replacement rates
  - Proposed SOFR rate provisions and variations
  - Definition of "Trigger Events"
- **Consent Requirements**:
  - Agent alone
  - Borrower
  - Majority Lenders
  - Requisite Lenders
  - Unanimous

Then, if we have a large portfolio of contracts containing a variety of different LIBOR Provisions and Replacement Rate Provisions all categorized in accordance with our Ontology, we can use the Ontology in a number of useful ways, including the following:

- Generate reports on how many loans in the portfolio contain each type of LIBOR Provision or Replacement Rate Provision
- Draft a form amendment for each type of interest rate provision using the data classifications in the Ontology, and then automatically generate an appropriate amendment.

It is much easier to input the data required for the Ontology one-by-one as loans are originated, than to try to sort through thousands of contracts consisting of unstructured data. If we start now to originate contracts as structured data and label the loan provisions in accordance with a detailed, standardized Ontology, then in theory we can completely eliminate the need to scan contracts, convert to text with OCR technology, and then use AI to categorize the loan provisions. Coding loans provisions up-front as loans are originated is 100% efficient, requires no AI, and is 100% accurate (subject only to human error in the drafting and coding process).

3.3.3. Optional Prepayments

We can also use a Chain to list the elements of a Legal Test in a particular order. This will be particularly useful when we develop a Legal Reasoner that needs to run through the elements of a legal test to see whether a Logic Equation is True or False. As a simple example, we can look at a typical section of a loan agreement authorizing optional prepayments. Breaking down the test into its component parts, we get the following:

Context	Chain Element
Who?	Borrower
Grant of Right	may
How?	upon notice to the Administrative Agent
When?	at any time and from time to time
What?	prepay any Borrowing in whole or in part without premium or penalty.

In this example, we have a Sentence with a Topic: Prepayment, Function: Grant of Right, and Short Name: Optional Prepayments. We can break down the Sentence into its component parts and store them as an Ordering Chain:

- [a: b: c: d: e:] = [Borrower: may: upon notice to the Administrative Agent: at any time and from time to time: prepay any Borrowing in whole or in part without premium or penalty.]

In the next two volumes in this Series, *The Logic of Legal Agreements – Building a Legal Reasoner* [Veatch Legal Reasoner 2021] and *The Mathematics of Language* [Veatch Math of Language 2021], we will explore structures like this in detail. For now, we just want to point out that in the future our Ontology will be able to store the elements of legal tests using the same Partition and Chain structures that we use for our Ontology of Sentences and abstract Ideas.

3.4. References, Historical Notes, and Further Reading

Math Without Numbers, [Veatch 2016]
The New Logic of the Law, [Veatch 2018]
Using the Logic of Lattices to Draw Inferences from Structured Data, [Veatch Inferences 2021]

4. RECEIVABLES PURCHASE AGREEMENTS

In this Chapter, we examine some of the provisions that are unique to a Receivables Purchase Agreement. As always, we start with our general template that we use for all contracts, and then add those provisions that are unique to Receivables Purchase Agreements.

4.1. Sentence Ordering Chain

In **Table 4-1**, we see some of the provision that are unique to a Receivables Purchase Agreement. For example, it is important to include a statement of Mutual Agreement as to whether or not True Sale treatment is intended by the parties.

Table 4-1 – Level Three Chain of Contract Provisions

	Level 1	Level 2	Level 3	Level 4
Title: RPA				
		...		
	Agreement			
		INTERPRETATION		
		RPA PROVISIONS		
			Facility	
			Advances	
			Commitment / Uncommitted	
			Term	
			[No] True Sale Treatment	
			Security Interest	
				Grant of Security Interest
				Perfection
				Power of Attorney
			Account Debtor Consent	
			Fees and Charges	
		...		
	Signatures			

4.2. Classification of Ideas (Other Than Sentences)

In this section, we set forth some of the Ideas that we need to flush out in any Ontology of Receivables Purchase Agreements, including whether the facility is recourse or nonrecourse; whether the agreement constitutes a True Sale of receivables; and whether the facility is committed or uncommitted.

4.2.1. Classification of Receivables Purchase Agreements

As always, we start with a Partition Equation.

Receivables Purchase Agreement $_{PE}$ =

Recourse: (Recourse + Nonrecourse) x

Sale: (True Sale + Recourse Factoring) x

Commitment: (Committed + Uncommitted) x

Governing Law: (New York + California + English + Other) x

Facility Size: (Small + Medium + Large) x

Receivable Size: (Small Ticket + Middle Market + Large Ticket) x

Account Debtors:

>**Jurisdiction:** (Domestic + Cross-Border) x
>
>**Entity Type:** (Private Corporation + Public Corporation + LLC + Government Entity) x
>
>**Industry:** (Healthcare + Shipping + Technology + Energy + Other $_{RE}$)

UCC Receivables Type: (Accounts + Instruments + Chattel Paper + General Intangibles)

The classification of the receivables is important under US law, because it can impact the proper means of obtaining a first priority, perfected security interest in the purchased receivables. For example, a lender or purchaser who takes possession or control of instruments or chattel paper, may have a priority security interest.

Also, receivables from a government entity typically require consent to assign.

Once again, we see that an Ontology can be an extremely helpful tool, provided, that we follow the steps for developing the Ontology:

- Determine what data we need to track.
- Create an Ontology reflecting the required data, including:
    - Attributes
    - The Range of Values for each Attribute
- Write a software application, *i.e.*, a Legal Reasoner, to sort and filter the contract data.

4.2.2. Timeline

For the Receivables Purchase Agreement Timeline, we look at the "offer and acceptance" process for receivables purchases to illustrate how we create a Timeline. In the case of a Receivables Purchase Agreement, there is usually a procedure that the parties follow, where:

- Seller submits to Buyer a pool of receivables for sale
- Buyer has a specified number of days in which to submit an offer to purchase
- Seller must accept or reject the offer within a specified number of days
- If Buyer's offer is accepted, then Buyer must fund within a specified number of days

These time periods can be specified in the Ontology as a classification of the possible dates and periods that are relevant in a receivables purchase transaction. Then, for any particular transaction, the parties select the relevant classification from the Ontology. Later, when a large portfolio of contracts has been originated, it is easy to sort and filter the Data to determine exactly what types of Contracts are in the portfolio.

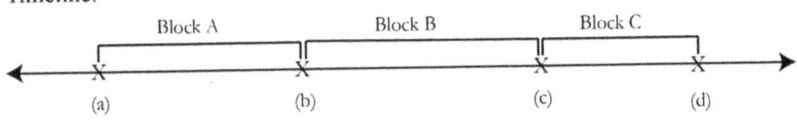

Fig. 4-1

4.3. References, Historical Notes, and Further Reading

Math Without Numbers, [Veatch 2016]

The New Logic of the Law, [Veatch 2018]

Using the Logic of Lattices to Draw Inferences from Structured Data, [Veatch Inferences 2021]

5. EQUIPMENT FINANCE AND LEASING

In an equipment lease, we have all of the issues that arise in a loan transaction, but in addition we have issues relating to the ownership of the equipment, including transfer of title, maintenance, insurance, and property tax.

5.1. Sentence Ordering Chain

Table 5-1 lists some of the lease-specific provisions that we need to flush out in our Ontology of equipment lease agreements.

Table 5-1 – Level Three Chain of Contract Provisions

	Level 1	Level 2	Level 3
Title: Equipment Lease Agreement			
	Caption		
	Recitals		
	Agreement		
		INTERPRETATION	
		LEASE PROVISIONS	
			Lease
			Rent
			No Lessor Warranties
			Equipment Maintenance
			Property Tax
		...	Sales Tax
			Insurance
			Return of Equipment
	Signatures		

5.2. Classification of Ideas (Other Than Sentences)

In this section, we look at the classification of equipment lease agreements, some unique issues regarding the Timeline, and the classification of Events of Default in an equipment lease.

5.2.1. Classification of Equipment Finance and Lease Agreements

Equipment leases can be either: (i) true leases which are governed by UCC Article 2A, or (ii) leases that create a security interest under UCC Article 9. We can use a Partition Equation to list the Attributes and Attribute Values that we use to classify leases.

Lease $_{PE}$ =

>**Lease Character**: (True Lease + Lease that Creates a Security Interest) x

>**True Lease** = (Finance Lease + $\neg$ Finance Lease)

The terminology for classifying leases can be confusing (and is somewhat in contradiction with accounting terminology), but a UCC True Lease can be either: (i) a Finance Lease, or (ii) a Lease that is not a Finance Lease.

5.2.2. Timeline

Equipment leases often have elaborate renewal and return provisions. The theory is that if the lessee is going to return the equipment, then the lessor needs time to arrange for remarketing of the equipment. Therefore, 30-90 days (or sometimes more) notice typically is required if the lessee is going to return the equipment. *See*, **Fig. 5-1** for an example of a lease Timeline.

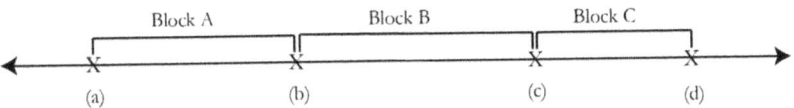

Fig. 5-1

5.2.3. Events of Default

Below is a Partition Equation for classifying the Events of Default in a typical equipment lease.

Event of Default $_{PE}$ =
(Payment Default + Non-Payment Lease Default + Financial Condition Default + Cross-Default + Fundamental Change in Business Default)

Payment Default $_{PE}$ = (Failure to Pay Rent + Failure to Pay Taxes + Failure to Pay Other Pre-Default Amounts + Failure to Pay Default Charges)

Failure to Pay Rent $_{PE}$ = (Interim Rent + Base Rent + Extension Rent + Holdover Rent)

Non-Payment Lease Default $_{PE}$ = (Breach of Representation + Immediate Default + Breach of Financial Covenant + Breach of Other Covenant + Seizure of Equipment)

Financial Condition Default $_{PE}$ = (Insolvency + Involuntary Insolvency Proceeding + Voluntary Insolvency Proceeding + Appointment of Receiver/Trustee + Material Adverse Change)

Cross-Default $_{PE}$ = (Lessor Cross-Default + Vendor Cross-Default + Real Property Lessor Cross-Default + Other Third-Party Cross-Default)

Fundamental Change in Business Default $_{PE}$ = (Merger or Consolidation + Sale of Assets + Other Change in Business)

In **Fig. 5-2**, is a visualization of the Event of Default classification.

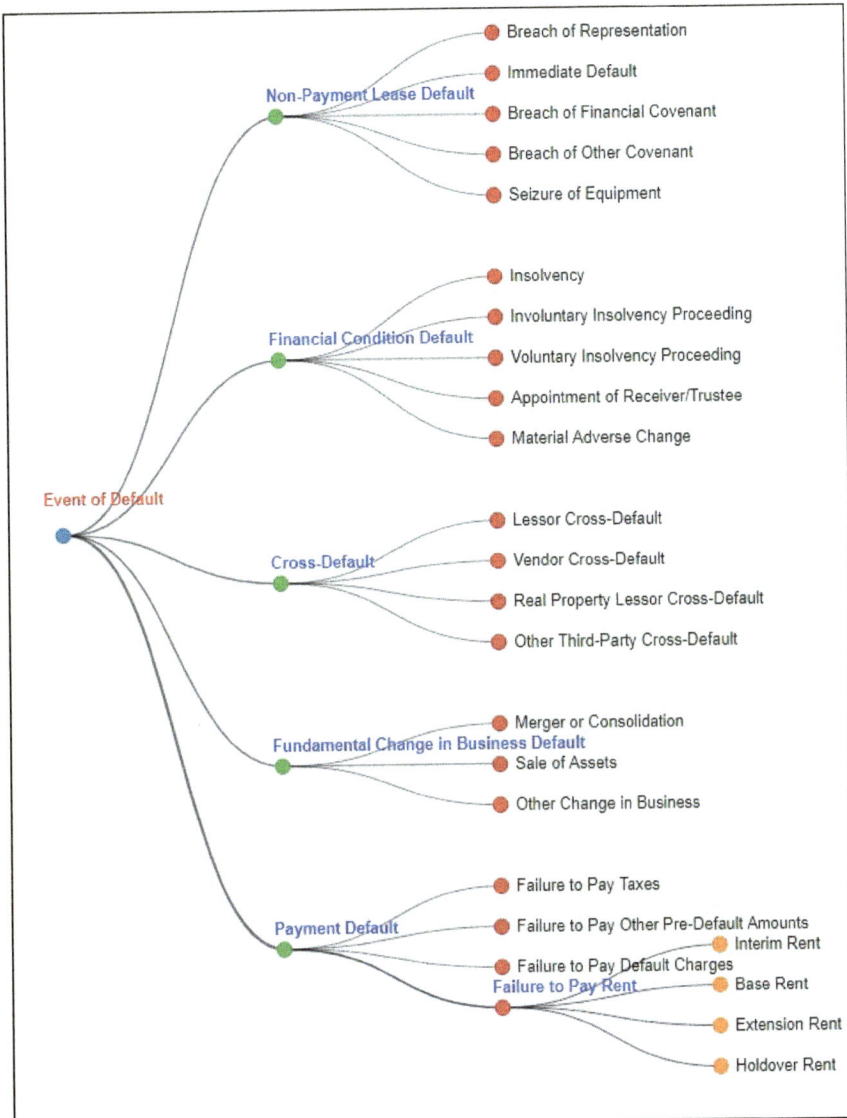

Fig. 5-2

5.3. References, Historical Notes, and Further Reading

Math Without Numbers, [Veatch 2016]

The New Logic of the Law, [Veatch 2018]

Using the Logic of Lattices to Draw Inferences from Structured Data, [Veatch Inferences 2021]

6. CONTRACT PORTFOLIO DATA

In this Chapter, we begin to look at the power of aggregating individual Contract Data in order to perform Data Analytics on large portfolios of Contracts. Once we have a standardized Ontology for Contract terms, we can easily aggregate portfolios of hundreds or thousands of contracts and perform Data Analytics on the portfolio.

6.1. Negotiations: Correlations Between Contract Terms and Customer Profiles

One use of Contract portfolio data is in the negotiation of Contracts. For example, if we want know what indemnification provision is standard for a customer of a certain profile, we can use our Ontology to identify customers that meet that profile and then find the corresponding indemnification provision as flagged and tagged using our standard Ontology.

6.2. Documentation: Comparison of Competing Contract Forms

Suppose Bank A is purchasing a loan portfolio from Bank B, but wants to know how Bank B's form loan agreement compares to Bank A's form loan agreement with respect to particular issues. A simple redline comparison of different forms often results in a completely unreadable mark-up. Comparing forms by searching for Topics, Functions, and Short Names, on the other hand, provides a means of honing in on the specific issue that we want to compare.

6.3. Monetization: Portfolio Diligence for Mergers & Acquisitions, Loans, or Securitizations

Perhaps the most beneficial use of a standardized Ontology is in the performance of due diligence on a large portfolio. A number of factors, including documentation risk, have an impact on the price that a buyer is willing to pay for a large portfolio of Contracts. Often, the buyer performs a "random spot check" on a sampling of Contracts in the portfolio, but it is simply not feasible from a cost perspective to review the entire portfolio. If, however, the Contracts in the portfolio were originated as Structured Data, then 100% of the Contract is available for sorting, filtering, and Logic Equation analysis using the Ontology.

6.4. Generation of Mass Amendments

Another use of Ontologies that is highlighted by the current LIBOR Transition crisis, is the creation of mass amendments. For Contracts originated in accordance with a detailed Ontology, there is no need to apply OCR to scan documents and then apply AI to categorize the Contract terms; the Contract terms were already flagged and tagged when the Contract was first created.

The current LIBOR Transition is a perfect example of a regulatory change that can give rise to a massive amendment project that could be simplified enormously if portfolios of contracts were already in a Structured Data format.

6.5. References, Historical Notes, and Further Reading

Math Without Numbers, [Veatch 2016]

The New Logic of the Law, [Veatch 2018]

Using the Logic of Lattices to Draw Inferences from Structured Data, [Veatch Inferences 2021]

7. CONCLUSION

Our goal has been to introduce the reader to the creation of an Ontology of the law, which is essentially a new field of study and practice in law that appears at the intersection of law and technology. This in turn will enable us to build a Legal Reasoner software application. We are at the threshold of truly transformative changes in the legal profession.

7.1. What We Have Learned About Creating an Ontology of Legal Contracts

In this book, we have endeavored to show how we can get started building an Ontology of Legal Contracts, with a focus on Finance Contracts. We started building an Ontology using a number of different types of building blocks or Atoms (in math terminology), including:

- Sentences
- Single Sets of Ideas
- Ordered Pairs of Ideas
- Ordered Triples of Ideas

For each type of Atom, we identified a number of different mathematical structures that are important when analyzing legal Contracts, including the following:

- **Sentences**
    o **Partitions (also known as an Equivalence Relations):** We created a Partition of Sentences by typical contract outline headings, *i.e.*, the Outline Structure.
    o **Ordering Chains (also known as an Order Relations):** We used an Ordering Chain to put the Sentences in the

order found in a typical contract.
- ○ **Attributes**: We used the Attributes of Topic, Function, and Short Name, among others, to classify and sort Sentences.
- **Single Sets of Ideas**
  - ○ **Objects**: We identified the Object Classification of Parties, Events on the Timeline, Representations, Covenants, Events of Default, and other Ideas that are found in a Contract.
  - ○ **Attributes**: For each Object, we can also create a list of Identifying Attributes.
  - ○ **Classification Chain**: We created a Classification Chain, which is characterized by the "is a" relationship, where each element "is a" member of each class that is higher up in the Chain.
- **Relations (Ordered Pairs):** We specified Relations between two Sets of Ideas, *i.e.*, Ordered Pairs (x,y), where xRy:
  - ○ **Relations**: Bank A "is a lender to" Company B
  - ○ **Inverse Relations**: The Inverse Relation is: Company B "is a borrower from" Bank A.
- **Ordered Triples**: We created Ordered Triples representing three party relationships, such as the following:
  - ○ Borrower, Lender, and Agent
  - ○ Borrower, Lender/Beneficiary, Guarantor
  - ○ Indemnitor, Indemnitee, Third-Party
  - ○ Vendor, Customer, Lender.

As a next step, we need industry leaders in lending, equipment leasing, and receivables finance to work on a proposal for a standardized Ontology of Finance Contracts.

In addition, we need experienced ontologists on the team, who understand the strengths and limitations of our current software data and reasoning technology. It would be extremely valuable, for example, to have a standardized data technology like RDF or OWL that implements the mathematics of Boolean Algebras that is required for a Legal Reasoner to use the Ontology to draw Inferences and perform over legal reasoning tasks. The current versions of semantic web technology were not designed with legal ontologies and legal reasoning in mind. Until the technology reflects the mathematics and the specifics of legal data, we will need experienced ontologists to assist in creating workarounds that preserve the integrity of the legal information.

This project needs to be a joint venture between experienced lawyers and experienced ontologists. We can create a much more valuable Ontology of the Law if we enlist the help of experienced attorneys in each specific area of expertise. In addition, we need experienced ontologists who understand: how the data will be used; what software tools are available to implement the Ongology; and how to visualize the data. In both cases, it is essential that the lawyers and ontologists understand the basic requirements of math and logic, so that we preserve and enable the ability to create legal reasoning software applications.

7.2. Questions to Ask Your Contract Management Solution Provider

When selecting a contract management software solution, it is important to address both (i) the short-term need to scan and convert documents to a machine-readable format, and (ii) the long-term goal of originating Contracts as Structured Data where the entire Contract is tagged with metadata. When evaluating contract origination and contract portfolio management solutions, here are some questions to ask the LegalTech provider.

Interim v. Long-Term Solution
- Is the software only an Interim Solution that (i) scans Contracts, (ii) applies OCR to create a machine-readable document, and (iii) uses AI to extract specific data points?
- How many data points can the software extract at a reasonable cost? Note that if we start with a form that is in a Structured Data format created with a detailed Ontology, then 100% of the Contract is tagged with metadata.
- Is the software also a Long-Term Solution that can originate Contracts in a 100% Structured Data format in accordance with a detailed Ontology?

Legal Advice from Qualified, Experienced Attorneys
- Does the Legal Tech company's product incorporate legal advice from experienced attorneys who are qualified in the applicable jurisdictions that are relevant to the Contracts in the portfolio?
  - If not, how do you ensure that quality legal advice is

reflected in the Contracts?

- When scanning a Contract portfolio, can the software identify quality issues such as the following?
    - Errors in logic
    - Errors in grammar
    - Ambiguous terms, *i.e.*, terms susceptible to two or more meanings
    - Unusual terms that resulted from unequal bargaining power in the negotiations
    - Manifest errors

- Can the software identify missing terms in the Contract?

- Does the software include an Ontology of the law? If so, who created the Ontology?

- What type of AI does the software use: "**Extraction AI**" or "**Legal Reasoning AI**"?
    - Does the software use AI to extract metadata from contracts, perform legal reasoning using math and logic, or both?
    - Is the software primarily a tool to assist human-led document review?
    - Alternatively, is the software a Legal Reasoner that can provide preliminary legal advice?
    - *E.g.*, can the software provide preliminary advice as to whether an Event of Default has occurred under a Contract?
    - Can the software generate a Compliance Memorandum, setting forth what the parties need to do to stay in compliance and avoid an Event of Default?
    - Can the software provide a Visualization of the Data?

- How does the software manage legal obligations of the parties to the contract that are found outside the four corners of the Contract, *e.g.*, in a statute such as the Uniform Commercial Code?

- Does the software analyze the impact of statutes, regulations, and case law generally?

The purpose of these questions is to highlight the need for quality control through a close collaboration between Law and Technology. If experienced lawyers create a Knowledge Representation Structure / Knowledge Base using a detailed, standardized Ontology of the Law, then the technology experts can create tools for sorting, filtering, and visualizing the legal information. Without quality legal Data classified in a standardized Ontology in accordance with the rules of math and logic, however, we cannot build a true Legal Reasoner AI software application.

7.3. Next Steps: Where Do We Go from Here?

We know how to create a standardized Ontology and companion Legal Reasoner. Now, we need to implement the technology through incremental and continuous improvement in processes.

1. **Create Standardized Ontology of Finance Contracts**: Industry leaders, including financial institutions, trade associations, technology companies, and law firms, need to collaborate to develop a standardized Ontology for Finance Contracts that is built upon a firm foundation in math and logic.

2. **Originate Contracts as Structured Data**: Once we have the Ontology, we should originate all new Contracts (including amendments to existing Contracts) as Structured Data in accordance with the Ontology.

3. **Convert Statutes to Structured Data**: Since many of the obligations of parties to Contracts are specified in, or limited by, statutes and regulations, we need to convert statutes and regulations to Structured Data well.

4. **Develop a Legal Reasoner**: Once we have the Data in a Knowledge Base constructed in accordance with the rules of math and logic, we can construct a true Legal Reasoner software application.

WILLIAM S. VEATCH

In the author's experience, once you are exposed to drafting Contracts as Structured Data and see the opportunities for Data Analytics and Visualization, there is no turning back.

WILLIAM S. VEATCH

BIBLIOGRAPHY

The year listed is the year of the latest revision by the author, but not necessarily the latest printing if no revisions were made. That way, the reader can get a sense of the historical perspective of the Book or article. (Note that the labels in the "Category" column form a valid Partition of the Book Titles!)

Abbreviation	Book	Category
[Aarts 2011]	Aarts, Bas, *Oxford Modern English Grammar*, Oxford University Press 2011.	Knowledge Base: English Grammar
[Abbott 1969]	Abbott, James C., *Sets, Lattices, and Boolean Algebras*, Boston, Allyn and Bacon, Inc. 1969.	Abstract Algebra
[Aldisert 1997]	Aldisert, Ruggero J., *Logic for Lawyers – A Guide to Clear Legal Thinking*, South Bend, IN, National Institute for Trial Advocacy 1997.	Legal Logic
[Allen 1984]	Allen, J.F., Towards a general theory of action and time. Artificial Intelligence 23, pp. 123-154. 1984. URL: http://dx.doi.org/10.1016/0004-3702%2884%2990008-0	Time
[Allen 1997]	Allen, J.F. and G. Ferguson, Actions and events in interval temporal logic In: Spatial and Temporal Reasoning. O. Stock, ed., Kluwer, Dordrecht, Netherlands, pp. 205-245. 1997. URL: http://dx.doi.org/10.1007/978-0-585-28322-7_7	Time
[Aluffi 2009]	Alluffi, Paolo, *Algebra: Chapter 0*, Providence, Rhode Island, American Mathematical Society 1990.	Abstract Algebra
[Aristotle 350 BCE]	Richard McKeon (ed.), *The Basic Works of Aristotle*, New York, Random House 1941.	Classical Logic.
[Arnold 1962]	Arnold, Bradford Henry, *Logic and Boolean Algebra*, Mineola, New York Dover 2011.	Logic
[Auslander and Buchsbaum 1974]	Auslander, Maurice and David A. Buchsbaum, *Groups, Rings, Modules*, Mineola, New York, Dover 1974.	Group Theory, Ring Theory
[Bachhuber 1957]	Bachhuber, Andrew H., *Introduction to Logic*, New York Appleton-Century-Crofts, Inc. 1957,	Logic
[Baynes 1861]	Baynes, Thomas Spencer, *The Port-Royal Logic*, London, Hamilton, Adams, and Co. 1861. Reprinted by Kessinger Legacy Reprints.	Logic
[Beason and Lester 2013]	Beason, Larry, and Mark Lester, *English Grammar and Usage*, New York, McGraw Hill 2013.	Knowledge Base: English Grammar
[Bergman 2012]	Bergman, Clifford, *Universal Algebra – Fundamentals and Selected Topics*, New York, CRC Press, 2012.	Abstract Algebra
[Birkhoff 1995]	Birkhoff, Garrett, *Lattice Theory*, Providence, Rhode Island, American Mathematical Society 1995.	Lattice Theory
[Birkhoff and	Birkhoff, Garrett, and Saunders Mac Lane,	Algebra

Abbreviation	Book	Category
[Mac Lane 1999]	*Algebra, 3d Ed.*, Providence Rhode Island, AMS Chelsea Publishing 1999.	
[Black 1952]	Black, Max, *Critical Thinking*, New Jersey, Prentice-Hall, 1952.	Logic
[Black 1968]	Black, Max, *The Labyrinth Of Language*, New York, Encyclopedia Britannica 1968.	Philosophy of Language
[Boole 1854]	Boole, George, *An Investigation of The Laws of Thought, On Which are Founded The Mathematical Theories of Logic and Probabilities*, New York, Dover Reprint of 1854 Ed.	Logic
[Bourbaki 1968]	Bourbaki, Nicolas, *Elements of Mathematics, Theory of Sets*, Menlo Park, California, Addison-Wesley Publishing Co. 1968.	Set Theory
[Brachman and Levesque 2004]	Brachman, Ronald J. and Hector J. Levesque, *Knowledge Representation and Reasoning*, San Francisco, California, Elsevier 2004.	Knowledge Representation
[Burris 1998]	Burris, Stanley, *Logic for Mathematics and Computer Science*, New Jersey, Prentice Hall 1998.	Logic
[Burris and Sankappanavar 1981]	Burris, Stanley and H.P. Sankappanavar, *A Course in Universal Algebra*, New York, Springer 1981.	Universal Algebra
[Burton 1970]	Burton, David M., *A First Course in Rings and Ideals*, Menlo Park, California, Addison-Wesley Publishing Company, Inc. 1970.	Ring Theory
[Cagle 2019]	Cagle, Kurt, The Power and Pitfalls of Inferencing, May 31, 2019 https://medium.com/swlh/the-power-and-pitfalls-of-inferencing-a07d06ef54e7	Inferencing
[Cameron 1994]	Cameron, Peter J., *Combinatorics: Topics, Techniques, Algorithsms*, Cambridge, Cambridge University Press 1994.	Combinatorics
[Carpineto and Romano 2004]	Carpineto, Claudio, and Giovanni Romano, *Concept and Data Analysis – Theory and Applications*, Chichester, West Sussex, England, John Wiley & Sons Inc. 2004.	Formal Concept Analysis
[Casanovas *et al.* 2012]	Casanova, Pompeu, Ugo Pagallo, Monica Palmirani, and Giovanni Sartor (Eds.), *AI Approaches to the Complexity of Legal Systems*, New York, Springer 2012.	AI and the Law
[Case, Funke, and Tortora 2016]	Case, Christine L., Berdell R. Funke, and Gerard J. Tortora, *Microbiology-An Introduction*, Essex, England, Pearson Education 2016.	Knowledge Base: Microbiology
[Caspard, Leclerc, and Monjardet 2012]	Caspard, Nathalie, Leclerc, Bruno, and Monjardet, Bernard, *Finite Ordered Sets*, New York, Cambridge University Press 2012.	Lattice Theory
[Cavender and Kahane 2014]	Cavender, Nancy, and Howard Kahane, *Logic and Contemporary Rhetoric*, 12th Ed., Boston, Massachusetts, Wadsworth Cengage Learning 2014.	Logic
[Chao ed. 1993]	Chao, Liu Hai, *Shaolin Gong-Fu – A Course in*	Knowledge

Abbreviation	Book	Category
	Tradition al Forms, Henan Scientific and Technical Publishing House 1994.	Base: Martial Arts
[Chen and Koh 1992]	Chen, Chuan-Chong and Koh, Khee-Meng, *Principles and Techniques in Combinatorics*, Singapore, World Scientific Publishing 1992.	Combinatorics
[Chilvers 2013]	Chilvers, Ian, Chief Consultant, *Art that Changed the World*, New York, Dorling Kindersley (DK) 2013.	Knowledge Base: Art
[CLA 2006]	Yahia, Sadok Ben, Engelbert Mephu Nguifo, Radim Belohlavek (Eds.), *Fourth International Conference, on Concept Lattices and Their Applications (CLA)*, New York, Springer 2008.	Lattice Theory
[Clark 1970]	Clark, Allan, *Elements of Abstract Algebra*, New York, Dover 1984.	Abstract Algebra
[Cogeval, Patry, and Guegan 2010]	Cogeval, Guy, Patry, Sylvie, and Guegan, Stephane, *Van Gogh, Gauguin, Cezanne, and Beyond*, New York, Del Monico Books -Prestel 2010.	Knowledge Base: Art
[Cogeval, Guegan, and Thomine-Barrada 2010]	Cogeval, Guy, Guegan, Stephane, and Thomine-Berrada, Alice, *Birth of Impressionism*, New York, Del Monico Books -Prestel 2010.	Knowledge Base: Art
[Cohn 1999]	Cohn, Paul M., *An Introduction to Ring Theory*, New York, Springer 2000.	Ring Theory
[Coile 2005]	Coile, D. Caroline, *Encyclopedia of Dog Breeds*, New York, Barron's 2005.	Knowledge Base: Dogs
[Copi 1973]	Copi, Irving M., *Symbolic Logic*, New York, Macmillan Publishing Co., Inc. 1973.	Symbolic Logic
[Cori and Lascar 1993]	Cori, René, and Daniel Lascar, *Mathematical Logic*, Oxford, Oxford University Press 2000.	Mathematical Logic
[Cothran Book I 2000]	Cothran, Martin, *Traditional Logic – Introduction to Formal Logic*, Memoria Press 2000.	Logic
[Cothran Book II 2000]	Cothran, Martin, *Traditional Logic – Advanced Formal Logic*, Memoria Press 2000.	Logic
[Cothran 2006]	Cothran, Martin, *Material Logic*, Memoria Press 2006.	Logic
[Couturat 1914]	Couturat, Louis, *The Algebra of Logic*, Chicago, The Open Court Publishing Company 1914.	Algebraic Logic
[Crawley and Dilworth 1973]	Crawley, P. and Dilworth, R.., *Algebraic Theory of Lattices*, New Jersey, Prentice-Hall, Inc. 1973.	Lattice Theory
[Curry 1976]	Curry, Haskell B., *Foundations of Mathematical Logic*, New York, Dover 1977.	Mathematical Logic
[Davey and Priestley 2001]	Davey, B.A., and Priestley, H.A., *Introduction to Lattices and Order (2d Ed.)*, Cambridge University Press 2002.	Lattice Theory
[DeLong 1998]	DeLong, Howard, *A Profile of Mathematical Logic*, Mineola, New York, Dover 1998.	Mathematical Logic
[De Morgan 1847]	De Morgan, Augustus, *Formal Logic: or, The Calculus of Inference, Necessary and Probable*, London, Taylor and Walton 1847. Reprinted by Scholar Select, 2017.	Logic
[Denney,	Denney, Joseph Villiers, Carson S. Duncan, and	Argumentation

Abbreviation	Book	Category
[Duncan, and McKinney 1910]	Frank C. McKinney, *Argumentation and Debate*, New York, American Book Company 1910. Reprinted by Forgotten Books 2012.	Argumentation and Debate
[Devlin 1993]	Devlin, Keith, *The Joy of Sets*, New York, Springer 1993.	Set Theory
[Dugundji 1966]	Dugundji, James, *Topology*, Boston, Allyn and Bacon, Inc. 1966.	Topology
[Ehrlich 1991]	Ehrlich, Gertrude, *Fundamental Concepts of Abstract Algebra*, Mineola, New York Dover 1991.	Abstract Algebra
[Enderton 1977]	Enderton, Herbert B., *Elements of Set Theory*, New York, Academic Press 1977.	Set Theory
[Ertel 2017]	Ertel, Wolfgang, *Introduction to Artificial Intelligence 2d Ed.*, Weingarten, Germany, Springer 2017.	Artificial Intelligence
[Evenden 1962]	Evenden, John. "A Lattice-Diagram for the Propositional Calculus." *The Mathematical Gazette*, vol. 46, no. 356, 1962, pp. 119–122. JSTOR, JSTOR, www.jstor.org/stable/3611637.	Lattice Theory
[Eves 1990]	Eves, Howard, *Foundations and Fundamental Concepts of Mathematics, 3rd ed.*, New York, Dover 1997.	Mathematics: Foundations
[Freeley and Steinberg 2009]	Freeley, Austin J., and David L. Steinberg, *Argumentation and Debate*, Boston, Massachusetts, Wadsworth Cengage Learning 2009.	Argumentation and Debate
[Frege 1879]	Frege, Gottlob, "Begriffsschrift, a formula language, modeled upon that of arithmetic, for pure thought" in *From Frege to Gödel, a Source Book in Mathematical Logic, 1879-1931*, Cambridge, Massachusetts, Harvard University Press 1967.	Mathematical Logic
[Frisch 1969]	Frisch, Joseph C., *Extension and Comprehension in Logic*, New York, Philosophical Library 1969.	Logic
[Funakoshi 1956]	Funakoshi, Gichin, *Karate-Do Kyohan – The Master Text*, New York, Kodansha International 1973.	Knowledge Base: Martial Arts
[Gamut 1991]	Gamut, L.T.F., *Logic, Language, and Meaning, Vol.1 Introduction to Logic*, Chicago, The University of Chicago Press 1991.	Logic
[Ganter and Wille 1999]	Ganter, Bernhard and Rudolf Wille, *Formal Concept Analysis*, New York, Springer 1999.	Formal Concept Analysis
[Ganter, Stumme, and Wille 2005]	Ganter, Bernhard, Stumme, Gerd, and Wille, Rudolf (Eds.), *Formal Concept Analysis – Foundations and Applications*, Springer 2005.	Formal Concept Analysis
[Gillie 1965]	Gillie, Angelo C., *Binary Arithmetic and Boolean Algebra*, New York, McGraw-Hill Book Company 1965.	Boolean Algebra
[Givant and Halmos 1998]	Givant, Steven and Paul Halmos, *Logic as Algebra*, The Mathematical Association of America 1998.	Logic
[Givant and Halmos 2009]	Givant, Steven and Paul Halmos, *Introduction to Boolean Algebras*, New York, Springer 2009.	Boolean Algebras and Rings
[Grätzer 2003]	Grätzer, George, *General Lattice Theory 2d Ed.*, Boston, Birkhäuser 2003.	Lattice Theory

WILLIAM S. VEATCH

Abbreviation	Book	Category
[Grätzer 2008]	Grätzer, George, *Universal Algebra 2d Ed.*, New York, Springer 2008.	Universal Algebra
[Halmos 1960]	Halmos, Paul R., *Naive Set Theory*, Princeton, Van Nostrand 1960.	Set Theory
[Halmos 1962]	Halmos, Paul R., *Algebraic Logic*, New York, Chelsea Publishing Company 1962.	Logic
[Hamilton]	Hamilton, George Heard, *The Library of Art History: 19th and 20th Century Art*, New York, Harry N. Abrams, Inc.	Knowledge Base: Art
[Hedman 2004]	Hedman, Shawn, *A First Course in Logic*, Oxford, Oxford University Press 2004.	Logic
[Hilbert and Ackermann 1938]	Hilbert, D. and W. Ackermann, *Principles of Mathematical Logic*, Providence, Rhode Island, AMS Chelsea Publishing 2008.	Mathematical Logic
[Hill and Leeman 1977]	Hill, Bill, and Richard W. Leeman, *The Art and Practice of Argumentation and Debate*, Mountain View, California Mayfield Publishing Company 1997.	Argumentation and Debate
[Hinman 2005]	Hinman, Peter G., *Fundamentals of Mathematical Logic*, Wellesley, Massachusetts, A K Peters 2005.	Mathematical Logic
[Hitzler and Schärfe 2009]	Hitzler, Pascal and Henrik Schärfe (Eds.), *Conceptual Structures in Practice*, Baca Raton, Florida, CRC Press 2009.	Formal Concept Analysis
[Hrbacek and Jech 1999]	Hrbacek, Karel, and Thomas Jech, *Introduction to Set Theory, 3d Ed.*, Boca Raton, Florida, CRC Press 1999.	Set Theory
[Huntington 1933]	Huntington, Edward V. "New Sets of Independent Postulates for the Algebra of Logic, With Special Reference to Whitehead and Russell's Principia Mathematica." *Transactions of the American Mathematical Society*, vol. 35, no. 1, 1933, pp. 274–304. *JSTOR*, JSTOR, www.jstor.org/stable/1989325.	Algebraic Logic
[Huntington 1937]	Huntington, Edward V. "Postulates for Assertion, Conjunction, Negation, and Equality." *Proceedings of the American Academy of Arts and Sciences*, vol. 72, no. 1, 1937, pp. 1–44. *JSTOR*, JSTOR, www.jstor.org/stable/20023279.	Algebraic Logic
[Hurley 2008]	Hurley, Patrick J., *A Concise Introduction to Logic, 10th Ed.*, Belmont, CA, Wadsworth Cengage Learning 2008.	Logic
[ICFCA 2004]	Eklund, Peter (Ed.), *Formal Concept Analysis, 2nd International Conference, International Conference on Formal Concept Analysis (ICFCA)*, New York, Springer 2004.	Formal Concept Analysis
[ICFCA 2009]	Ferré, Sébastien, and Sebastian Rudolph (Eds.), *Formal Concept Analysis, 7th International Conference, ICFCA*, New York, Springer 2009.	Formal Concept Analysis
[ICFCA 2011]	Valtchev, Petko, and Robert Jäschke (Eds.), *Formal Concept Analysis, 9th International Conference, ICFCA*, New York, Springer 2011.	Formal Concept Analysis

Abbreviation	Book	Category
[ICFCA 2012]	Domenach, Florent, Dmitry I. Ignatov, Jonas Poelmans (Eds.), *Formal Concept Analysis, 10th International Conference, ICFCA,* New York, Springer 2012.	Formal Concept Analysis
[ICFCA 2013]	Cellier, Peggy, Felix Distel, Bernhard Ganter (Eds.), *Formal Concept Analysis, 11th International Conference, ICFCA,* New York, Springer 2013.	Formal Concept Analysis
[ICFCA 2014]	Glodeanu, Cynthia Vera, Mehdi Kaytoue, Christian Sacarea (Eds.), *Formal Concept Analysis, 12th International Conference, ICFCA,* New York, Springer 2014.	Formal Concept Analysis
[Isaacs 2008]	Isaacs, I. Martin, *Finite Group Theory*, Providence, Rhode Island, American Mathematical Society 2008.	Group Theory
[Jackson 1985]	Jackson, Philip C., *Introduction to Artificial Intelligence 2d Ed.*, New York Dover Publications, Inc. 1985.	Artificial Intelligence
[Jech 2003]	Jech, Thomas, *Set Theory – 3d Millennium Ed.*, New York Springer 2003.	Set Theory
[Jevons 1877]	Jevons, W. S., *Elementary Lessons in Logic*, Macmillan and Co. 1877. Reprint by Forgotten Books.	Logic
[Jurix 2000]	Ed., *Legal Knowledge and Information Systems*, Washington, DC, IOS Press 20	AI and the Law
[Jurix 2001]	Ed., *Legal Knowledge and Information Systems*, Washington, DC, IOS Press 20	AI and the Law
[Jurix 2002]	Bench-Capon, Trevor, Aspassia Daskalopulu, Radboud Winkels Eds., *Legal Knowledge and Information Systems, JURIX 2002: The Fifteenth Annual Conference, Foundation for Legal Knowledge Systems*, Washington, DC, IOS Press 2002.	AI and the Law
[Jurix 2003]	Ed., *Legal Knowledge and Information Systems*, Washington, DC, IOS Press 20	AI and the Law
[Jurix 2004]	Ed., *Legal Knowledge and Information Systems*, Washington, DC, IOS Press 20	AI and the Law
[Jurix 2005]	Moens, Marie-Francine and Peter Spyns Eds., *Legal Knowledge and Information Systems*, Washington, DC, IOS Press 2005.	AI and the Law
[Jurix 2006]	Ed., *Legal Knowledge and Information Systems*, Washington, DC, IOS Press 20	AI and the Law
[Jurix 2007]	Ed., *Legal Knowledge and Information Systems*, Washington, DC, IOS Press 20	AI and the Law
[Jurix 2008]	Ed., *Legal Knowledge and Information Systems*, Washington, DC, IOS Press 20	AI and the Law
[Jurix 2009]	Ed., *Legal Knowledge and Information Systems*, Washington, DC, IOS Press 20	AI and the Law
[Jurix 2010]	Ed., *Legal Knowledge and Information Systems*, Washington, DC, IOS Press 20	AI and the Law
[Jurix 2011]	Ed., *Legal Knowledge and Information Systems*, Washington, DC, IOS Press 20	AI and the Law
[Jurix 2012]	Ed., *Legal Knowledge and Information Systems*, Washington, DC, IOS Press 20	AI and the Law
[Jurix 2013]	Ed., *Legal Knowledge and Information Systems*,	AI and the Law

Abbreviation	Book	Category
	Washington, DC, IOS Press 20	
[Jurix 2014]	Hoekstra, Rinke Ed., *Legal Knowledge and Information Systems*, Washington, DC, IOS Press 2014.	AI and the Law
[Jurix 2015]	Ed., *Legal Knowledge and Information Systems*, Washington, DC, IOS Press 20	AI and the Law
[Jurix 2016]	Ed., *Legal Knowledge and Information Systems*, Washington, DC, IOS Press 20	AI and the Law
[Kaburlasos 2006]	Kaburlasos, Vassilis G., *Towards a Unified Modeling and Knowledge-Representation based on Lattice Theory*, New York, Springer 2006.	Lattice Theory
[Kamke 1950]	Kamke, E., *Theory of Sets*, New York, Dover 1950.	Set Theory
[Klammer, Schulz, and Volpe 2013]	Klammer, Thomas P., Muriel R. Schulz, and Angela Della Volpe, *Analyzing English Grammar 7th Ed.*, New York, Pearson Education, Inc. 2013.	Knowledge Base: English Grammar
[Kleene 1967]	Kleene, Stephen Cole, *Mathematical Logic*, Mineola, New York, Dover 1967.	Mathematical Logic
[Klenk 1994]	Klenk, Virginia, *Understanding Symbolic Logic, 3d.*, Englewood Cliffs, New Jersey, Prentice Hall 1994.	Logic
[Kneale and Kneale 1971]	Kneale, William, and Martha Kneale, *The Development of Logic*, Oxford, Clarendon Press 1971.	Logic
[Kneebone 1963]	Kneebone, G. T., *Mathematical Logic and the Foundations of Mathematics*, New York, D. Van Nostrand Company Ltd. 1963.	Mathematical Logic
[Kolln, Gray, and Salvatore 2016]	Kolln, Martha, Loretta Gray, and Joseph Salvatore, *Understanding English Grammar*, New York, Pearson 2016.	Knowledge Base: English Grammar
[Kneebone 1963]	Kneebone, G.T., *Mathematical Logic and Foundations of Mathematics*, New York, D. Van Nostrand Company Limited 1963.	Mathematical Logic
[Kreeft 2010]	Kreeft, P., *Socratic Logic*, South Bend, Indiana, St Augustine's Press 2010.	Logic
[Kunen 2011]	Kunen, Kenneth, *Set Theory*, London, College Publications 2011.	Set Theory
[Langer 1966]	Langer, Susanne K., *An Introduction to Symbolic Logic*, New York, Dover 1967.	Logic
[Lawvere and Rosebrugh 2003]	Lawvere, F. William, and Rosebrugh, Robert, *Sets for Mathematics*, University of Cambridge 2003.	Set Theory
[Levy 1979]	Levy, Azriel, *Basic Set Theory*, Mineola, New York, Dover 1979.	Set Theory
[Lipschutz 2012]	Lipschutz, Seymour, *General Topology*, New York, McGraw Hill 2012.	Topology
[Lukasiewicz 1957]	Lukasiewicz, Jan, *Aristotle's Syllogistic 2d Ed.*, Oxford, Clarendon Press 1957.	Logic
[Margaris 1967]	Margaris, Angelo, *First Order Mathematical Logic*, Waltham, Massachusetts, Blaisdell Publishing Company 1967.	Mathematical Logic
[Maritain 1946]	Maritain, Jacques, *Formal Logic*, New York, Seed &	Logic

Abbreviation	Book	Category
	Ward 1946.	
[Markman 1998]	Markman, Arthur B., *Knowledge Representation*, New York, Psychology Press 1998.	Knowledge Representation
[McInerny 2004]	McInerny, Dennis, *La Logique Facile*, Paris, Eyrolles 2004.	Logic
[Mill 1872]	Mill, John Stuart, *System of Logic Vol. II*, London, Longmans, Green, Reader, and Dyer 1872. Reprint by Forgotten Books 2012.	Logic
[Minto 1893]	Minto, William, *Logic – Inductive and Deductive*, Boston, Adamant Media 2005. (Unabridged facsimile of the edition published in 1893 by John Murray, London.)	Logic
[Moore 2013]	Moore, Gregory H., *Zermelo's Axiom of Choice*, Mineola, New York, Dover 2013.	Set Theory
[Monk 1969]	Monk, J. Donald, *Introduction to Set Theory*, New York McGraw-Hill, Inc. 1969.	Set Theory
[Monk 1989]	Monk, J. Donald Ed., *Handbook of Boolean Algebras, Vol. 1-3*, Elsevier Science Publishers B.V. 1989.	Boolean Algebra
[Northcott 1968]	Northcott, D.G., *Ideal Theory*, Cambridge University Press 1968.	Ring Theory, Ideal Theory
[Parker and Veatch 1959]	Parker, Francis H. and Henry B. Veatch, *Logic as a Human Instrument*, New York, Harper & Brothers 1959.	Logic
[Parrochia and Neuville 2013]	Parrochia, Daniel and Neuville, Pierre, *Towards a General Theory of Classifications*, Springer Basel, 2013.	Universal Logic, Classification Theory
[Pinter 1990]	Pinter, Charles C., *A Book of Abstract Algebra*, 2d ed., Mineola, New York, Dover, 1990.	Abstract Algebra
[Pinter 2014]	Pinter, Charles C., *A Book of Set Theory*, Mineola, New York, Dover 2014.	Set Theory
[Porphyry 260 C.E.]	Porphyry, *Introduction*, Translated by Jonathan Barnes, New York, Oxford University Press 2003.	Logic
[Potter 2009]	Potter, Michael, *Set Theory and its Philosophy*, Oxford University Press 2009.	Set Theory
[Quine 1969]	Quine, Willard Van Orman, *Set Theory and Its Logic*, Cambridge, Massachusetts, Harvard University Press 1969.	Set Theory, Logic
[Quine 1981]	Quine, Willard Van Orman, *Mathematical Logic*, Cambridge, Mass., Harvard University Press, 1981.	Mathematical Logic
[Quine 1982]	Quine, Willard Van Orman, *Methods of Logic*, Cambridge, Massachusetts, Harvard University Press 1982.	Logic
[Quine 1986]	Quine, Willard Van Orman, *Philosophy of Logic*, Cambridge, Massachusetts, Harvard University Press 1970.	Logic
[Read 1909]	Read, Carveth, *Logic – Deductive and Inductive*,	Logic

Abbreviation	Book	Category
	London, Alexander Moring Limited 1909. Reprinted by Forgotten Books 2012.	
[Rees 2012]	Rees, Martin Ed., *Universe*, New York, Dorling Kindersley (DK Smithsonian) 2012.	Knowledge Base: Space Science
[Rigdon 1903]	Rigdon, Jonathan, *Grammar of the English Sentence*, London, Forgotten Books 2013.	Knowledge Base: Astronomy and the Planets
[Rodgers 2000]	Rodgers, Nancy, *Learning to Reason*, New York, John Wiley & Sons, Inc. 2000.	Set Theory, Logic
[Roman 2008]	Roman, Steven, *Lattices and Ordered Sets*, New York, Springer 2008.	Lattice Theory
[Russell 1920]	Russell, Bertrand, *Introduction to Mathematical Philosophy*, New York, Dover ed. 1993.	Philosophy
[Russell 1921]	Russell, Bertrand, *The Analysis of Mind*, Mineola, New York, Dover 2005.	Philosophy
[Russell and Whitehead 1910]	Russell, Bertrand, and Alfred North Whitehead, *Principia Mathematica Vol. 1-3*, Rough Draft Printing 2011.	Logic
[Salmon 2013]	Salmon, Merrilee H., *Introduction to Logic and Critical Thinking*, 6th Ed., Boston, MA, Wadsworth, Cengage Learning 2013.	Logic
[Schmidt 2011]	Schmidt, Gunther, *Relational Mathematics*, Cambridge, Cambridge University Press, 2011.	Relations
[Schröder 2003]	Schröder, Bernd S. W., *Ordered Sets*, Boston, Birkhauser 2003.	Lattice Theory
[Shenefelt and White 2013]	Shenefelt, Michael, and Heidi White, *If A, then B - How the World Discovered Logic*, New York, Columbia University Press 2013.	Logic
[Shertzer 1986]	Shertzer, Margaret D., *The Elements of Grammar*, New York, Macmillan Publishing Company 1986.	Knowledge Base: English Grammar
[Sikorski 1964]	Sikorski, Roman, *Boolean Algebras*, New York, Springer-Verlag 1964.	Boolean Algebra
[Sider 2010]	Sider, Theodore, *Logic for Philosophy*, Oxford, Oxford University Press 2010.	Logic
[Singh 1959]	Singh, Jagjit, *Great Ideas of Modern Mathematics: Their Nature and Use*, New York, Dover Publications 1959.	Mathematics
[Smullyan 1968]	Smullyan, Raymond M., *First-Order Logic*, New York, Dover Publications 1995.	Mathematical Logic
[Smullyan 2014]	Smullyan, Raymond M., *A Beginner's Guide to Mathematical Logic*, New York, Dover Publications 2014.	Mathematical Logic
[Solomon 1990]	Solomon, A. D., *The Essentials of Boolean Algebra*, 1990.	Boolean Algebra
[Sowa 1984]	Sowa, John F., *Conceptual Structures: Information*	Knowledge

Abbreviation	Book	Category
	Processing in Mind and Machine, Menlo Park, California, Addison-Wesley Publishing Company 1984.	Representation
[Sowa 2000]	Sowa, John F., *Knowledge Representation*, Pacific Grove, California, Brooks/Cole 2000.	Knowledge Representation
[Stewart 2004]	Stewart, Ian, *Galois Theory*, New York, Chapman & Hall/CRC 2004.	Galois Theory
[Stewart and Tall 1977]	Stewart, Ian and Tall, David, *The Foundations of Mathematics*, Oxford University Press 1977.	Set Theory
[Stoll 1963]	Stoll, R.R., *Set Theory and Logic*, New York, Dover 1963.	Set Theory
[Stone 1936]	Stone, M.H., "The Theory of Representation for Boolean Algebras," Trans. Amer. Math. Soc. **40**, 37-111 (1936).	Boolean Algebras
[Stone 1937]	Stone, M.H., "Applications of the Theory of Boolean Rings to General Topology," Trans. Amer. Math. Soc. **41**, 375-481 (1937).	Boolean Algebras
[Sullivan 2005]	Sullivan, Scott M., *An Introduction to Traditional Logic*, North Charleston, SC, Booksurge Publishing 2006.	Logic
[Suppes 1972]	Suppes, Patrick, *Axiomatic Set Theory*, New York, Dover 1972.	Set Theory
[Tall 2014]	Tall, Aliou, *From Mathematics in Logic, to Logic in Mathematics*, Boston, Docent Press 2014.	Logic
[Thurman 2003]	Thurman, Susan, *The Only Grammar Book You'll Ever Need*, Avon Massachusetts, Adams Media 2003.	Knowledge Base: English Grammar
[Tiles 1989]	Tiles, Mary, *The Philosophy of Set Theory*, Mineola, New York, Dover 1989.	Set Theory
[Toth 2020]	Toth, Herbert, *Relations: Concrete, Abstract, and Applied – An Introduction*, Toh Tuck Link, Singapore, World Scientific Publishing co. Pte. Ltd., 2020.	Relations
[Toulmin 2003]	Toulmin, Stephen E., *The Uses of Argument*, New York, Cambridge University Press 2008.	Argumentation
[Toulmin, Rieke, and Janik 1979]	Toulmin, Stephen, Richard Rieke, and Allan Janik, *An Introduction to Reasoning*, New York, Macmillan Publishing Co. 1979.	Argumentation
[van der Waerden 1966]	Van der Waerden, B.L., *Algebra Vol. I*, New York, Springer 1970.	Abstract Algebra
[van der Waerden 1967]	Van der Waerden, B.L., *Algebra Vol. II*, New York, Springer 1970.	Abstract Algebra
[Veatch 2016] or [MWN Vol. 1]	Veatch, William S., *Math Without Numbers: The Mathematics of Ideas, Vol. 1 Foundations*, Createspace (2016), available on Amazon.com.	Boolean Algebra, Logic
[Veatch 2017]	Veatch, William S., *Propositional Logic as a Boolean Algebra – A New Perspective*, Createspace (2017),	Boolean Algebra, Logic

Abbreviation	Book	Category
	available on Amazon.com.	
[Veatch Inferences 2021]	Veatch, William S., *Using the Logic of Lattices to Draw Inferences from Structured Data*, Amazon (2021).	Knowledge Base: Ontologies
[Veatch JELF 2018]	Veatch, William S., "Using Artificial Intelligence Technology to Remain Competitive in a Fintech Environment," Journal of Equipment Lease Financing (2018).	AI and the Law
[Veatch Series 2018]	Veatch, William S., Series: "Applying the Mathematics of Ideas and the Logic of Lattices to Understand the Categorical Syllogism of Classical Logic," Createspace (2018), Books 1, 2, 3, and 4 available on Amazon.com.	Boolean Algebra, Logic
[Veatch NLOL Vol.1 2018]	Veatch, William S., *The New Logic of the Law Vol. 1 – Building a Foundation for Artificial Intelligence in the Law*, Createspace (2018), available on Amazon.com.	Law, Logic
[Venn 1894]	Venn, John, *Symbolic Logic*, London, Macmillan and Co., Forgotten Books ed. 2012.	Logic
[Vladimirov 1994]	Vladimirov, D. A., *Boolean Algebras in Analysis*, Boston, Kluwer Academic Publishers 2002.	Boolean Algebra
[Wallace 1998]	Wallace, D.A.R., *Groups, Rings and Fields*, London, Springer 1998.	Group Theory, Ring Theory
[Walton 2016]	Walton, Douglas, *Argument Evaluation and Evidence*, New York, Springer 2016.	Argumentation
[Warren 2013]	Warren, Rebecca, Knowledge Encyclopedia, New York, Dorling Kindersley (DK Smithsonian) 2013.	Knowledge Base: General
[Whately 1836]	Whately, Richard, *Elements of Logic*, New York, William Jackson 1836.	Logic
[Whitesitt 1960]	Whitesitt, J. Eldon, *Boolean Algebra and Its Applications*, Mineola, New York, Dover 2010.	Boolean Algebra
[Whitney 1933]	Whitney, Hassler. "Characteristic Functions and the Algebra of Logic." *Annals of Mathematics*, vol. 34, no. 3, 1933, pp. 405–414. JSTOR, JSTOR, www.jstor.org/stable/1968168.	Algebraic Logic
[Willard 1970]	Willard, Stephen, *General Topology*, Mineola, New York, Dover 1970.	Topology

Index

Page numbers in parenthesis refer to pages in Volumes of the "Math Without Numbers" series of books. "MWN1" refers to *Math Without Numbers – Vol. 1 Foundations* [Veatch 2016]. "PL1" refers to *Propositional Logic as a Boolean Algebra – A New Perspective* [Veatch 2017]. "NLOL1" refers to *The New Logic of the Law Vol. 1* [Veatch 2018]. "Inferences" refers to *Using the Logic of Lattices to Draw Inferences from Structured Data*, [Veatch 2021].

A Argument (NLOL1 6) Argument by Analogy (NLOL1 6) Atom, (MWN1 9) Atomic Formula, (PL1 67) Attribute, (MWN1 10), 1 Attribute Element, (PL1 12, 37, 44) Attribute Labels (NLOL1 16, 163) Attribute Lattice, (PL1 13) Attribute Signature, (MWN1 177) Attribute Statement, (Inferences 3)	**D** Dataset (NLOL1 135) Declarative Sentence, (PL1 139) Deemed Atom (NLOL1 14) Direct Product, (MWN1 129) Disjoint, (MWN1 78, 94) Domain, (MWN1 46, 254, 261, 266, 272)
B Base Set, (MWN1 130) Boolean Algebra, (MWN1 131) Boolean Lattice, (PL1 54-55)	**E** Element (NLOL1 17, 19) Empty Set (NLOL1 21) Equal (NLOL1 38) Equivalence Class, (MWN1 29, 32) Equivalence Relation, (MWN1 22, 113) Euler Diagram, (MWN1 15) Exhaustive, (MWN1 190) Extension, (MWN1 10) Extent, (MWN1 21)
C CBNF, (PL1 3, 69) Chain, (MWN1 169), 3 Classical Logic, (MWN1 16) Composition of Functions, (Inferences 115) Composition of Relations, (Inferences 75) Compound Argument (NLOL1 79) Compound Idea, (MWN1 9) Cover, (MWN1 84) Cover Plus a Difference, (MWN1 45)	**F** False (NLOL1 29) Filter, (MWN1 108, 132) Finite, (MWN1 62) First Order, (PL1 2) Formal Concept Analysis (NLOL1 13, 177)
G Galois Theory, (MWN1 121) Group, (MWN1 303)	**M** Map (NLOL1 27) Mathematical Logic (NLOL1 175) Mathematics of Ideas (NLOL1 21) Mutually Exclusive, (MWN1 26) MWN, (MWN1 i)

	MWN1, (PL1 231)
	MWN Propositional Logic, (PL1 xi)
H	**N**
Hasse Diagram, (MWN1 310)	Natural numbers, (MWN1 262)
Heterogeneous Relation, (Inferences 90)	New Logic of the Law (NLOL1 2)
Hierarchy Tree, (MWN1 207)	NLOL (NLOL1 136)
Homogeneous Relation, (Inferences 90)	Normal Form, (PL1 67)
I	**O**
Idea, (PL1 15)	Object, (MWN1 10), 1
Inferences, (Inferences 2)	Object Labels (NLOL1 136)
Infinite, (MWN1 62)	Ontology, 1
Inheritance, (MWN1 40)	Order, (MWN1 73)
Inverse Relation, (Inferences 75)	Ordered by Inclusion (NLOL1 3)
"Is a" Relation, (MWN1 252)	Ordered Pair (NLOL1 27), 3
Isomorphic, (PL1 15)	Ordered Triple (NLOL1 27)
K	
Knowledge Base, 2	
Knowledge Representation Structure (NLOL1 27), 2	
L	
Lattice, (MWN1 73)	
Lattice Element, (PL1 2)	
Lattice Position, (PL1 27, 139, 149)	
List Set, (MWN1 24)	
Literal, (PL1 67)	
Logic (NLOL1 25)	
Logic Formula, (PL1 179)	
Logic of Lattices, (PL1 12)	

P	**T**
Pairwise Disjoint, (MWN1 192)	Test Set, (MWN1 27)
Paradoxes,	Third Order, (PL1 3)
Russell's, (MWN1 277)	Topology, (MWN1 311)
Partially Overlapping (NLOL1 38)	True, (PL1 21, 23, 181)
Partition, (MWN1 190) (Inferences 13-14), 3	Truth Equation (NLOL1 81)
	Truth Value, (PL1 21, 23, 181)
Partition Equation, (MWN1 153, 202), (Inferences 96)	Two-Set Relationship, (PL1 121)
	Two-Set Relationship Clause, (Inferences 3)
Partition Set, (PL1 139, 181)	
Power Set, (MWN1 9, 122)	
Power Set Boolean Algebra, (Inferences 73)	
Power Set Contraction, (MWN1 50, 151, 268)	
Power Set Expansion, (MWN1 50, 151, 268)	
Predicate, (PL1 121)	
Predicate Logic (NLOL1 101)	
Proposition, (MWN1 7, 11)	
Propositional Logic (NLOL1 66)	

R	**U**
Relation, 1, 3 Relation Algebra, (Inferences 74) Relation-Proposition Map, (Inferences 89) Relative Complement, (MWN1 85) Ring, (MWN1 308)	UCC (NLOL1 15) Uniform Commercial Code (NLOL1 15) Union, (MWN1 81, 102) Universe of Discourse (U_D), (PL1 21, 23, 118) Up Set, (MWN1 108, 144), (NLOL1 34) Up Set of Inheritance (NLOL1 125)
S	**V**
Set, (MWN1 54 *et seq.*) Single Sets, 3 Subset (NLOL1 21) Superset (NLOL1 26) Superset-Subset Relationship (NLOL1 124) Syllogism, (MWN1 8, 11, 16)	von Neumann, (MWN1 256, 284)

WILLIAM S. VEATCH

ABOUT THE AUTHOR

William S. Veatch is a practicing attorney and partner at the global law firm Norton Rose Fulbright US LLP, living in San Francisco, California. He obtained his B.A. degree in History at the University of Winnipeg, Winnipeg, Manitoba, Canada (1985), where he also studied Mathematics and Philosophy; his LL.B. law degree at the University of Manitoba, Winnipeg, Canada (1985); and his J.D. law degree from the University of California, Hastings College of the Law, San Francisco, California (1987).

In addition to his debt, equipment leasing, and receivables finance/securitization practice, Bill works with the Innovation team at Norton Rose Fulbright US LLP, where he creates Ontologies of the Law, converts Contracts to Structured Data, and develops software applications for processing Data from Contracts and Statutes.